The People and Culture of
Japan

Conversations Between
Donald Keene and Shiba Ryotaro

Translated by
Tony Gonzalez

Japan Publishing Industry Foundation for Culture

Note on Japanese names

All Japanese names appearing in this book are given in Japanese order, with family name first.

The People and Culture of Japan: Conversations Between Donald Keene and Shiba Ryotaro
Donald Keene and Shiba Ryotaro. Translated by Tony Gonzalez.

First published 2016
by Japan Publishing Industry Foundation for Culture (JPIC)
3-12-3 Kanda-Jinbocho, Chiyoda-ku, Tokyo 101-0051, Japan

Paperback edition: 2018

© 1972, 2013 by Donald Keene, Uemura Yoko and Shiba Ryotaro Memorial Foundation
English translation © 2016 by Japan Publishing Industry Foundation for Culture
All rights reserved

This book is a complete translation of *Nihonjin to nihonbunka* from the Collected Works of Donald Keene, Vol. 9; *Donarudo kiin chosakushu dai 9 kan: sekai no naka no nihonbunka* (Shinchosha Publishing Co., Ltd., 2013), which is also in print since its original publication in 1972 as a book published by CHUOKORON-SHINSHA, Inc. Its contents comprise three conversations held in 1971, respectively at the Nara Hotel, the Ginkakuji temple in Kyoto, and the Tekijuku Academy in Osaka.

Jacket and cover design: Niizuma Hisanori
Front and cover photo © Umehara Shoichi

Printed in Japan
ISBN 978-4-86658-048-7
http://www.jpic.or.jp/japanlibrary/

JAPAN LIBRARY

Foreword to the English Edition

The following dialogues took place in 1971, and were first published in Japanese in 1972. Over forty years have passed since then, yet they seem as pertinent today as they did back then. Indeed, they provoke quiet reflection upon the fundamental origins of Japan in this time of troubles.

This year marks the twentieth anniversary of Shiba's passing. In this milestone year, we look forward to the English translation of these dialogues as a new opportunity for many people to come to better know Japan. Shiba Ryotaro devoted his life to consideration of Japan and its people, so I'm sure that he would have been equally thrilled.

Uemura Yoko
Director
Shiba Ryotaro Memorial Foundation
February, 2016

Preface to the English Edition

My share of *The People and Culture of Japan* began with a telephone call from an editor who informed me of a crisis. Shiba Ryotaro, the most popular writer in Japan, had agreed to participate in a dialogue for his magazine, but the scholar who was scheduled to be Shiba's counterpart in the dialogue had been stricken with illness. The editor asked if I would serve as his substitute. My first response was to refuse on the grounds that I had not read Shiba's books and felt unqualified to engage in a dialogue with him. The editor called again, this time to say that Shiba had requested that I not read his books. This unexpected, rather humorous command changed my mind and I gladly accepted.

Shiba made one request—he asked that the place of our conversations not be outside the Kansai region. He lived near Osaka and for this reason might not have wished to travel far from home. Or perhaps he had already conceived the dialogue in terms of how one section of the country had reflected the different epochs of Japanese history. In any case, our meetings took place in Nara, Kyoto, and Osaka.

We met at the site of the Heijo palace in Nara, the earliest capital of Japan. The ruins were scant and not very suggestive of the remains of a castle, but that evening, during our conversation in the hotel, Shiba revealed that the ruins had evoked in him the dawn of Japanese civilization. He articulated with such eloquence what Japan must have been like in ancient times that I thought I would have nothing to add. That night, after our dialogue had ended, I could not recall having said anything to Shiba. It was only after reading the proofs that it became apparent that Shiba had in fact asked questions that he knew would interest me. Nervousness had made me think I had said hardly a word, but he had actually enabled me to say quite a lot.

The second dialogue was at Ginkakuji temple in Kyoto. It just so happened that it took place on a cold winter night. Special permission had been obtained to keep the buildings open after the usual closing time. Shiba, however, was sensitive to the cold, and as soon as the necessary photographs were taken we hurried out of Ginkakuji and headed for a heated restaurant.

The third was the dialogue I enjoyed most. Shiba and I walked together along Midosuji avenue in Osaka, stopping at monuments that were related to Matsuo Basho who had died nearby. We ate dinner at a restaurant, said to be several hundred years old, where we shared tables with other people in the old style. I no longer felt the tension that had hovered over me during the two preceding meetings and we talked like old friends. We would remain friends from then until his sudden death.

I have one fault to find with this book. I believe that Shiba was overly kind and generous in what he wrote about me. I am not a genius, nor am I the best scholar of Japanese literature. I am grateful for the friendship revealed in such words of praise, but I have become too modest a Japanese to accept them.

Donald Keene
September, 2015

Table of Contents

Foreword to the English Edition **3**

Preface to the English Edition **5**

Preface **9**

CHAPTER 1
The Birth of Japanese Culture **13**

CHAPTER 2
Kukai, Ikkyu, and the Universality of Religion **31**

CHAPTER 3
The World of Gold, the World of Silver: The Aesthetics of
Troubled Times **47**

CHAPTER 4
The Japanese View of War **63**

CHAPTER 5
Confucianism and Japanese Morals **77**

CHAPTER 6
Westerners in Japan **97**

CHAPTER 7
Japanese Morals, Revisited **125**

CHAPTER 8
The Culture of Edo **143**

Afterword **161**

About the Authors **165**

Preface

If I were forced to define my relationship with Donald Keene, then despite our shared experience of war taking place on opposite sides of an ocean, I would have to call him a comrade-in-arms. I unfortunately remain unsure as to exactly what meaning the war held for me, but there is one thing I know: were it not for that war, the world of Japanese culture would have been lessened by never having acquired the genius of Donald Keene.

My first meeting with Keene was one of varied strange impressions. Despite his already being old enough to be graying at the temples, I had never before met an individual whose appearance as a youth I could so easily reconstruct in my mind. He had delicate eyelashes like the down on a baby bird, and below that, eyes always ready to sparkle with childlike curiosity. He seemed to have a flame burning inside that immediately distilled the tidbits captured by his inquisitive and sensitive intellect into purer truths. That flame, which has burned like an eternal votive candle, first lit in the dim light of a New York subway when Keene was a student, peering at a notebook of Japanese characters he'd collected and wondering about their odd attraction and the culture that lay beyond them. War dragged that youth toward a fate of Japanese language studies. Without the war, he never would have ended up performing the task of applying universality to that unique corner of humanity known as Japanese culture.

It was my fate to be born Japanese. My birth was registered in the city hall of a Japanese town, and by virtue of this alone I became part of the nation called Japan. From this I have deluded myself into thinking that I know something about the country. Many other Japanese people no doubt share the same delusion, and I'm sure that, like myself, they are startled from time to time when confronted with their misapprehension. The source of such disquiet is frequently a work by Donald Keene.

It was Shimanaka Hoji, chairman of the publishing house Chuokoron-Sha, who suggested that I meet and have a conversation with Keene. My initial impulse was to refuse, unable to imagine taking on such a daunting task. In Japan I am known as a writer, but that label has been applied by others rather than by me; indeed, it is one I have long avoided. I have never even stopped to consider whether what I write is fiction or non-fiction, and I am well aware that any attempt to do so would likely result in my no longer being able to write in my own words. For one thing, I know next to nothing about the history of Japanese literature. I am nowhere near brave enough to attempt writing novels—or anything like them—from beneath the crushing weight of the accumulated strata of Japanese literature, and so have strived to safeguard my mind from such knowledge. Donald Keene, on the other hand, not only has a deep grasp of and exquisite appreciation for Japanese literature, but is an erudite scholar who has taken on the Herculean task of writing down its complete history.

So I came back to Mr. Shimanaka with a self-serving condition: "Only if he'll avoid talking about Japanese literature."

This was an unfair burden to place on Keene, I know, but thankfully he responded positively, and the result is the series of conversations recorded in this book. I pressed Mr. Shimanaka with a further request: "If we can arrange for some artificial happenstance, I'd like to do so. Namely, I would like the setting to be a conversation between two men of similar age, both with an interest in the people and culture of Japan, who are chatting after having met by chance on a city street."

Again, Mr. Keene received this well.

We met on a cold day at the site of Heijo palace in Nara. That was our first meeting, at least; that evening we drank together at our hotel, and later met again at Ginkakuji temple in Kyoto. This second meeting was at night, after the tourists had left, and beyond the rock gardens a sickle moon floated in an indigo sky. It almost felt as if the publisher had arranged for this spectacular backdrop as the perfect setting for our discussions. Our third meeting took place atop the age-browned tatami mats of Tekijuku, the nineteenth-century Osaka academy famous for popularizing Western studies at the end of the Edo period. Our conversation that day continued on the second floor of Maruji, a small restaurant in Semba. I am an Osaka native, but Keene's knowledge of local personages such as seventeenth-century bunraku puppet theater playwright Chikamatsu Monzaemon and poet Ihara Saikaku far exceeded my own, making me a poor representative of my hometown.

"We're near the place where Basho died, aren't we?" he once said, setting up the local to act as tour guide for the Basho scholar. I had vague memories from junior high school of seeing a small commemorative plaque to that effect on a Midosuji avenue street corner, near the site of the old Hanaya residence. After some wandering along Midosuji, I was quite relieved to spot the plaque in a patch of greenery beside the sidewalk.

"Ah, here we are," I said, to which Keene murmured, "Indeed." He kneeled down for a closer look, and I lit several matches to provide some feeble illumination—my only significant contribution to Keene's Basho studies.

I stood by the side of the road, hoping to hail a taxi to take us to Osaka's north district, yet failing to notice that every car passing by was headed south. It was Keene who pointed out my error: "Shiba-san, isn't this now a one-way street?" he said. Mortified at being corrected by a New Yorker, I mumbled something along the lines of, "Ah yes, I remember reading about that in the newspapers," and dragged him off to another location. Walking through the Semba district, which was nearly deserted at that time of night, I felt as if we were wandering

in a forest. We finally made our way to a street with traffic heading
north, but I'm sure I succeeded in impressing Keene with my amaz-
ingly poor sense of direction. Bona fide tax-paying resident of Osaka
though I may be, thus is the extent of my ability to guide a visitor along
the streets of my own city. Need I say more about my hesitation to conduct anyone through Japanese culture, a common property shared by
all humanity?

I will say, however, that I thoroughly enjoy speaking with people,
and my conversations with Donald Keene were even more enjoyable
than most.

According to an essay by Ichihara Toyota, the poet and former
French ambassador to Japan Paul Claudel once spoke the following
words to philosopher Paul Valéry at a dinner party: "One race that I
certainly hope will not die out is the Japanese. I know of no other people with such an interesting, ancient culture, and I am not at all surprised by their recent advances. They may be poor, but they are noble."

This occurred in the autumn of 1943, a time when Japan's even-
tual defeat had become evident, as well as the year both Keene and
myself were dragged into the war. These of course would have been
sweet words to my ears, and given Keene's knowledge and emotions
regarding the Japanese-speaking world—which go beyond even those
of most Japanese—I have no doubt he would have welcomed the sentiment as well. However, the following conversations were conducted
in Japanese, and the inherent reticence of that language restrained us
from overindulgence in such sweet phrases. I hope instead that what
follows in printed form conveys our mutual warmth toward Japanese
culture.

Shiba Ryotaro
from his home in eastern Osaka

CHAPTER 1

The Birth of Japanese Culture

Japan's Desire for Esteem

Shiba   Today we're in Nara, and we've just toured the site of Heijo palace. Back when that palace was new[1], Japan was a country with just a scattering of rice paddies and no real commodities. It was a poor nation covered mostly in meadows and forests, so it's rather impressive to me that its inhabitants managed to build such a grand capital. I suppose the goal was, in modern terms, to present something like an international exposition?

Keene   Yes, I think that's probably right. The first large temple built in Japan was Shitennoji[2], but I believe it served largely as a place to receive foreign visitors, likely from China. It was a way of showing people from more advanced countries that Japan had its own culture, that it too could build splendid temples. A similar sentiment was probably a significant motivation behind building Heijo palace. People were likely worried that otherwise, Japan would be seen as a backward, barbarian nation. Along the same lines, we also see literary works from that period conveying a very strong message that Japan had a history and culture too, like the *Nihon Shoki* (The Chronicles of Japan)[3], the

---

1. Nara became the national capital in 710.
2. Established by Prince Shotoku in 593.
3. One of the oldest books of Japanese mythical and historical records.

14   Chapter 1

Man'yoshu[4], and the Chinese-language poetry compilation *Kaifuso*[5].

So the Japanese have been quite conscious of foreigners since ancient times, and worried that they might be looked down upon or made fun of. The same thing happened again in the Meiji era, with the Rokumeikan Hall and all the Victorian-style buildings intended to show that Japan was just as culturally evolved as any other country. I believe Heijo palace served a similar role, given that if we consider only the domestic situation there was little need for such a splendid capital.

Shiba   They say it was exactly half the size of the palace at Chang'an[6], which would make it quite large indeed. The population of Chang'an was said to be over one million back then, so you can imagine the need for a large palace. The city supposedly had restaurants and bars and Persian merchants and the like walking about, but Heijo was nothing like that. There were no bars or anything else that would make it feel like a place where the common folk lived. Most importantly, no remains of toilets have been found. What other evidence could better show that no one actually lived there? [Laughs]

Also, people from other lands were summoned to the Chang'an palace for coronations and other important ceremonies, right? The Chinese would put on ceremonial dances and the like for these guests, and host ceremonies to show that China abided by the Confucian ideals of *li*[7]. Including foreigners in these ceremonies was an important element of Chinese culture, and the Japanese felt they had to mimic this practice, too.

Keene   When we visited the Heijo palace museum today we saw an

---

4. The oldest existing collection of Japanese-language poetry, compiled in the Nara period.
5. The oldest collection of Chinese poetry by Japanese authors, compiled by an unknown figure in 751.
6. Modern-day Xi'an, the capital of Shaanxi province, China.
7. Confucian ideals related to rituals, customs, and etiquette.

The Birth of Japanese Culture   15

object commemorating the arrival of a dignitary from Balhae[8]. At the time, the Chinese Tang dynasty was considered the center of the world, with people from all corners visiting to pay tribute to its court. I suppose the Japanese needed something similar in order to maintain their self-respect. No doubt they were thrilled to receive tribute from Balhae.

Shiba   Of course paying tribute wasn't the whole story. When ministers from various countries came to the Tang palace they would receive reciprocal gifts worth two or three times the value of what they had brought. That positioned China as the senior partner in the relationship, like the head of the family. Conversely, by receiving those gifts the visitors were acknowledging that they were dependent, that they were the branch off the family tree. But there was a nice payoff for that in what the ambassadors got to take home. I guess receiving gifts isn't always an easy thing to do.

Keene   Yes, to the point that even China started asking countries to stop bringing so much tribute all the time! [Laughs]

Shiba   I don't know whether Balhae's emissaries visited Japan in an attempt to please court officials, but they came often. So like China, Japan started to request that they not visit quite so much. Japan was a poor country and couldn't afford to repay double or triple what it received. Maybe the court could manage this two or three times, but beyond that visitors started to become a burden. Actually, there were very few ethnic groups in the Japanese region at the time. The Japanese even considered the Hayato people of southern Kyushu to be a different ethnicity, as evidenced by the Hayato shields we saw in the museum today.

Keene   Or so they wished to believe…

---

8. Balhae was a nation that existed in southeastern Manchuria and the northern part of the Korean peninsula between the eighth and tenth centuries.

16   Chapter 1

Shiba   The customs of the Hayato were considered very exotic, so the court would call them in to participate in ceremonies. There was another group of people from the Kuzu area beyond Mt. Yoshino who would be summoned to perform the *kuzu-no-mai* ritual dance, but the Hayato people didn't really have any artistic skills other than imitating dogs[9]. Anyway, it seems that Japan was imitating the customs of other countries, if on a smaller scale. As to why they would want to do such a thing, I suppose it's as you say, the Japanese foreign consciousness.

Even the Taika Reform[10] wouldn't have happened if Emperor Yang of Sui hadn't unified the continent first. The shock of that incident provoked reforms in Japan and got people thinking that Japan should be unified too. A number of years later the magnificent culture of the Tang dynasty arose, and once again Japan had to do something similar. Surely it would have been easier to succumb to the Tang as a subject nation, but the intervening ocean not only prevented Chinese invasions, it also made travel to China difficult. So perhaps the Japanese decided to reproduce a miniature version of China on their own soil.

Keene   That was likely the case. Otherwise, why would the Japanese go to the trouble of creating collections of poetry in the Chinese language, like the *Kaifuso*? They must have known from the beginning that the task was nearly impossible, but nevertheless they had to show that Japan's culture was comparable to China's.

By the way, I'm not sure what the situation was in the Nara period, but some resistance to the previous dominance of Chinese culture definitely emerged in the early Heian period. This is particularly evident around the time of Sugawara no Michizane (845–903). Of course, I think you could say that this complex love–hate relationship with

---

9. The Hayato people were famous for using dog-like barking sounds in rituals to placate evil spirits.

10. A series of reforms by Emperor Kotoku in 645 aimed at centralizing power in the imperial court, following the Chinese model.

Chinese culture is precisely what eventually gave rise to the unique culture of Japan.

Shiba   A moment ago you mentioned that Shitennoji temple served as a kind of guesthouse, right? Well, modern-day Osaka sits on solid ground, but back then most of today's Osaka was ocean. The only land was the Uemachi Plateau, where Shitennoji and Osaka Castle are located, so the first thing Chinese ships entering Osaka Bay would have seen was that guesthouse. The Japanese who built it probably wanted to make visitors say, "We've been turning up our noses at Japan all this time, but look at this!"

There's a famous story from around that time in which Prince Shotoku sends Emperor Yang of Sui a diplomatic letter addressed "From the Sovereign of the Land of the Rising Sun to the Sovereign of the Land of the Setting Sun." Emperor Yang must have thought the Japanese were impertinent, ignorant barbarians to address the lord of all lands in such a manner. Still, China's emissaries would have had quite the reception at Japan's official guesthouse. It's interesting to think about Japanese culture developing from this delicate posturing. On the surface the Japanese looked like they were entertaining superiors, but in reality they were adopting the posture of an equal.

Japanese Acceptance of Foreign Culture

Keene   When you look at Japan's history, you can see from all angles a relation of love and hate, of acceptance and rejection of foreign cultures. In *The Tale of Genji*, for example, the descriptor "Tang-like" means "foreign," but it's used in a derogatory manner. I believe the word originally had positive connotations, but to my understanding here it's negative. Specifically, it connotes a garish style unbecoming for Japan. In the same book there are also instances of deference to Chinese culture, but then again you have this resistance. That's one

18   Chapter 1

of the things that makes *The Tale of Genji* such an invaluable work of literature.

If you look at the ancient literature of Korea, or much later that of Vietnam, the novels mostly take place in China. People just didn't write many books about their own countries. The protagonists in Vietnamese novels are generally Chinese. The same is true in Korean novels. But in Japanese novels, while some stories might take place in China—*Hamamatsu Chunagon Monogatari* (The Tale of Middle Counselor Hamamatsu)[11], for example—the stories themselves are about Japan. There's this feeling that the Japanese too are worthy of appearing in drama, that they too experience sorrows and joys worth writing about. That's the spirit in which the *Man'yoshu* was written.

Much later, in the mid-Edo period, I think it was the poet and nativist philosopher Kada no Azumamaro (1669–1736) who called the *Man'yoshu* the *Shijing* (Classic of Poetry)[12] of the East. I'm sure people of the Nara period thought the same thing, that just as China had its *Shijing*, Japan had the *Man'yoshu*, so they were no barbarian nation.

Shiba   I agree. Along the same lines, Sei Shonagon had a wonderful sense of Chinese-influenced stylishness, which you can see in her *Makura no Soshi* (Pillow Book)[13]. I imagine her as "Tang-like" in a very refined way, slender and stylish. So the sense of "Tang-like" meaning "putting on airs" is the pendulum swinging back the other way.

Keene   I don't know enough Korean to say this with authority, but I don't imagine there's an equivalent to the expression "Tang-like"

---

11. An eleventh-century tale by an unknown female author about a Japanese Imperial counselor who travels to China after learning that his father has been reincarnated as a Chinese prince.
12. The oldest existing collection of Chinese poetry, dating from the eleventh to the seventh centuries BC.
13. A collection of musings and observations from a court lady of Heian-period Japan.

in Korean literature. It's hard to imagine them expressing the same kind of antipathy toward Chinese culture that we see in the Japan of that time.

Shiba   By the late Silla period in Korea[14], a movement to adopt Chinese systems was well underway. Before that Koreans had Korean-language names, but around that time they started taking on names derived from Chinese, like Syngman Rhee and Park Chung-hee. This was quite unusual. I believe the Vietnamese and their language were much more similar to the Han Chinese to start with. So the Vietnamese people were already speaking a similar language, but Korean had very different linguistic roots. For that reason you wouldn't have expected them to adopt Chinese names, but starting in the late Silla period there was this all-encompassing shift to Confucian systems, including bureaucratic institutions and the like. This peaked in the Joseon dynasty, which lasted for over five hundred years, all the way up to the early twentieth century. So for over five centuries every aspect of life was permeated with Chinese culture. Even writing was done in Chinese. Present-day Koreans are very proud of their hangul alphabet, which developed around Japan's Muromachi period (1337–1573), but hangul started out as something for women, children, and the illiterate, a vulgar symbolic representation of "real" characters. So other than *Chunhyangjeon* (The Story of Chunhyang)[15], not much of what we would call literature was written in Korean.

In Japan too, around the time of *The Tale of Genji* only people of low stature used the native kana syllabary exclusively, but in Korea hangul was considered distinctly vulgar. There was no intellectual demand for literature written in hangul, so poems or songs in hangul didn't stick around; they weren't recorded or preserved. No collections like the

---

14. Approximately the seventh through the eighth centuries.
15. One of the best-known Korean folktales.

20   Chapter 1

Man'yoshu or Japan's tanka love poems exist from that era. It seems that just as the political systems of Korea had been engulfed by China, so had its literature.

Keene   The most dangerous period for Japan must have been the century after the Nara period, around the ninth century by the Western calendar. The popularity of Chinese literature peaked at that time, so it wouldn't have been surprising if Japanese literature had faded away. But for whatever reason Japan's literature instead grew stronger, and despite the danger it had faced at one point, around the end of the ninth century and the beginning of the tenth we get literary works like *Taketori Monogatari* (The Tale of the Bamboo Cutter)[16] and the *Kokinshu* (The First Imperial Anthology of Japanese Poetry)[17]. Had things turned out differently, a situation similar to that in Korea and Vietnam might have developed, with people feeling that literature should be written in Chinese while Japanese should just be used for giving orders to ignorant servants. I believe that the reason things didn't turn out that way—or one of the reasons, at least—has to do with the issue of male and female social status.

Specifically, in the Japan of that time women held high positions in court, but as a rule they did not study Chinese. Well, actually some did... The story goes that although *The Tale of Genji* author Murasaki Shikibu wasn't directly taught Chinese, she listened in on her brother's lessons, and being smarter than him she actually learned them. In any case, in a society where the men learned Chinese and the women didn't, a man who wanted to express his desires to a woman in writing would of course have to do so in a comprehensible form. I wonder if that isn't how waka poetry became popularized. Just giving gifts

---

16. The oldest known Japanese narrative folktale.
17. An abbreviation of *Kokin Wakashu*, a collection of Japanese waka poetry from the Heian period.

or flowers would have been extremely poor etiquette; you also had to express your feelings in writing. Doing so in Chinese wouldn't get you anywhere, so you'd write a poem in Japanese instead. [Laughs]

Shiba An acquaintance suggested that I read the Chinese poems of Sugawara no Michizane in that light, and doing so was quite interesting. They read very much like an "I-novel" confessional work. It was actually Yukawa Hideki (1907–1981)[18] who pointed this out, which prompted me to read them, and I thought, "Ah, I see. He's expressing his grief after having lost a son named Amaro…"

Keene Ah, that one.

Shiba You know it? He describes this sadness that refuses to leave him. Chinese poets are a bit more masculine than that. Of course there were all kinds of Chinese poets, but like Michizane they were the scholar-gentry, and therefore a kind of model for masculinity, which is reflected in their poetry. So you might expect Michizane to express grief in his poems in some reserved form, but he releases this thick torrent of emotion. That feels surprisingly Japanese to me, and something that Chinese poetry is not well suited to expressing. Perhaps Japanese was better for such tender, meandering language.

Keene I believe so. For example, *Tosa Nikki* (The Tosa Diary) is considered one of the first classics of Japanese-language literature. Its author Ki no Tsurayuki (868?–945?) opens the book with a phrase along the lines of, "It is usually a man who keeps what's called a diary, but here a woman will see what she can do." So he's seeing what it's like to keep a diary as a woman. As to why he would do such a thing, he was a man, and the governor of Tosa[19] no less, so writing about unmanly things wouldn't have been fitting. So he adopts this little fiction. Of

---

18. Theoretical physicist and first Japanese recipient of the Nobel prize.
19. Present-day Kochi prefecture.

course he could have written in Chinese if he had chosen to, but then he wouldn't have been able to express the feelings he really wanted to get out. In particular, his favorite child, a young daughter, had died in Tosa, and that's the theme of the entire work. He should have been happy to get back to his home in Kyoto, but without his daughter he felt only loneliness. There was no enjoyment to be had. I believe *that's* what he wanted to say more than anything, and why he wrote the diary in the first place. It wouldn't have been possible if he were writing in Chinese.

Shiba   I suppose some things were just difficult to express in Chinese. Perhaps this is an overly bold thing to say, but maybe the ancient Japanese learned about masculinity through Chinese language, while our underlying archetype is feminine. What do you think?

Keene   I think that's a fine thing for a Japanese person to say, but as a foreigner it would be dangerous for me to say the same. [Laughs]

"Masculinity" and "Femininity"

Shiba   Of course, when I say the Japanese are archetypically feminine I don't mean that in a disparaging way, or that it's some kind of problem. I find that people with a certain kind of constancy and bravery are often feminine types who tend to stick to their ideals and stubbornly maintain what is right, while more masculine types are likely to spin on their heels and head off in another direction. And while I may be getting off topic, it seems like many great military leaders—both now and in the past, and in the East and the West as well as Japan—have been on the feminine end of the spectrum. For Chinese examples consider Zhang Liang (?–186 BC)[20], or more recently Lin Biao, both of whom I

---

20. An advisor to Emperor Gaozu of Han and instigator of the Western Han rebellion that toppled the Qin dynasty.

think had very feminine personalities. In the West, Wellington wasn't exactly a manly man, by which I mean the kind of man you see in old cowboy movies. Even Napoleon would be considered more feminine than masculine in that regard.

Of course I'm making crude generalizations here, but I'm talking about a kind of core strength, not weakness. I'm saying that so far as methods of expressing love and the like go, the archetypical Japanese, or perhaps I should say the early Japanese, have this strong feminine feel to them.

Keene   A number of poems in the *Man'yoshu* have a very masculine feel to them. Even Otomo no Yakamochi (718?–785) wrote poems like that. But by the period of the *Kokin Wakashu* you don't see much of that anymore. I suppose Japanese poets did become more feminine. After a period during which male poets tried to present a masculine appearance, men and women entered an era of writing exactly the same kind of thing. Determining the sex of the author from the text alone becomes nearly impossible. In some cases men even wrote as women. Ki no Tsurayuki is just one example, although I don't know any examples of women writing as men.

Shiba   Neither do I.

Keene   Certainly neither Sei Shonagon nor Murasaki Shikibu tried to present themselves as men. [Laughs]

Shiba   They were quite proudly women! Changing the subject again but staying in the same vein, around the time of Basho (1644–1694) masculinity suddenly reappears in Japanese literature. Of pre-Meiji poets, Basho and Saigyo (1118–1190) strike the deepest chord with me, but Saigyo has more of this sense of femininity. His birth name was Sato Norikiyo, and he was a big guy, a noble warrior in service to Retired Emperor Toba. He was reportedly a skilled archer, which

24   Chapter 1

seems manly enough, but his poems in the *Kokin Wakashu* have a definite feminine air. The poems of Basho, on the other hand, feel very masculine to me. What do you think?

Keene   I agree. For one thing, when you read Basho's haiku you never see the word "I." He takes a very impartial, objective viewpoint. You almost never see him writing in a subjective, feminine style. I'm sure, of course, that even as a man he was emotionally moved by things, but he never writes, "*I* wet *my* sleeves with tears." He was extremely masculine, writing in the style of great poets like the Tang dynasty's Du Fu (712–770). I mention Du Fu, but when you speak of Chinese poets in Japan I suppose Bai Juyi (772–846) comes to mind first, which is another case of the feminine side being more prominent. But you don't see that in Du Fu's poems at all. I don't think there's ever been a more masculine poet. I feel like you have to get up to Basho before you can truly appreciate Du Fu.

Shiba   Well now that's interesting. Yes, the Japanese hold Bai Juyi and his collection—was it *Baishi Wenji*?—in quite high esteem. When I read his poems I think, let's see… Well, I recall one about a public servant posted to some countryside town. He's single and lonely. He plants a rose in his hedge and tells it, "If you'll bloom, I'll make you my wife." Such emotion doesn't quite feel like proper Chinese poetry, not as I normally consider it. It feels more Japanese.

Keene   The Chinese consider him a great poet, but I don't think any of them would call him the best.

Shiba   Do you think there was something about Basho that made him understand Du Fu on a fundamental level?

Keene   I don't think Basho would agree with everything Du Fu said, but he did quote him in his *Oku no Hosomichi* (The Narrow Road to

Oku): "Countries may fall, but their rivers and mountains remain—"

Shiba   "—when spring comes to the ruined castle, the grass is green again."

Keene   Basho lay his bamboo hat on the ground, sat on it, and composed a famous haiku:

> *The summer grasses—*
> *Of brave soldiers' dreams*
> *The aftermath*

Here he's in good agreement with Du Fu. But just a little earlier he had visited Taga castle and upon seeing a stele there wrote precisely the opposite: "Mountains crumble and rivers disappear, new roads replace the old, and stones are buried and vanish in the earth." In other words, in time mountains will come down and rivers will dissipate, so what will remain? Well, as evidenced by this ancient tablet, human words, that's the main thing. Even when the mountains and rivers are gone and the grasses have dried up, our words remain. That's what he said. When I read that, I was truly moved. In *The Narrow Road to Oku* he quotes that line by Du Fu, "Countries may fall, but their rivers and mountains remain," and writes what is arguably his greatest haiku, the one about summer grasses. But at the same time he sees this stele, and considers that there is something even more eternal than mountains and rivers—words, he writes. I think that's just wonderful.

Shiba   When I visited the Mogami river it happened to be a rainy day. It was the wet season too, which reminded me of another famous Basho haiku:

> *Gathering seawards*
> *The summer rains, how swift it is!*
> *Mogami river*

I understand that your visit to the Mogami river wasn't so fortunately timed?

Keene   Yes, I seem to take rain with me everywhere I go, but on that particular day it was beautiful out. [Laughs]

Shiba   If we compare the "masculinity" and "femininity" of contemporaries in Japanese literature since the Meiji era, it's interesting to look at Natsume Soseki and Masaoka Shiki, who were friends. These two appeared just as modern Japanese literature was developing—you might even say that they developed it—but I'd say that Shiki was the feminine type and Soseki the more masculine. Personally, I don't think Shiki's haiku and tanka are all that great, but his prose is wonderful.

Keene   I agree entirely.

Shiba   When Soseki was relatively young, he used to tease Shiki. "Your writing is so frail," he said, "you can't seem to shake this womanly style," and, "Just keep writing, day in and day out, like a child practicing his letters." I believe that was from a letter Soseki wrote around 1889. And Shiki just kept on writing, which I think puts him in the feminine camp.

Keene   But I'd bet that Shiki considered himself the very personification of manliness.

Shiba   I'm sure he did, which makes it all the more interesting. When he was young he was a radical who attended Freedom and People's Rights Movement speeches, and even gave a few himself, so as you say he probably only recognized his own "masculine" side. He came to Tokyo with the intent of some day becoming prime minister, after all. Not that he was the type to take on such a role, by any stretch of the imagination. He entered a college prep school but kept failing the entrance exams because his English was so poor, and ended up pursuing a Japanese literature degree. Not because that's what he wanted to study, but because that's all his English ability allowed for. So he finally got into a Japanese literature program, but studying that alone wasn't enough for him. He wanted to introduce Western aesthetics and trigger a literary revolution, a reevaluation of haiku. So there's another masculine approach to things.

When the First Sino–Japanese War occurred, Shiki wanted nothing more than to join the military. Everyone around him was worried about his illness[21], but he insisted. At the time he was a reporter for the newspaper *Nippon*, and when its president Kuga Katsunan finally gave in and allowed him to enlist, Shiki wrote, "This is the most wonderful event of my life." So while his life appears to have overflowed with masculinity, his literary works are all quite feminine.

Keene   All of the foreign works he liked were quite masculine too. Benjamin Franklin's autobiography, for example, and Smiles' *Self-Help* were particular favorites. I wonder if his lack of interest in beautiful literature and novels, despite his reading of foreign literature, was due to the cult of success that characterized the Meiji era.

Shiba   As I believe you have written somewhere before, it's poignant to imagine Shiki on his deathbed, still reading and being moved by Franklin. He would surely never regain an active life, and in fact was likely to die soon, yet he continued to read and be excited by Franklin's glorious deeds.

Keene   Right. Franklin's autobiography is full of phrases like "early to bed, early to rise" that embody the spirit of the West, but such admonitions were worthless to an invalid like Shiki. It's extremely sad, if anything.

---

21. Shiki suffered from tuberculosis for most of his life.

28   Chapter 1

Shiba   When Shiki left Matsuyama Middle School and entered college prep school, he was friends with Akiyama Saneyuki, a boy from his hometown who was also in preparatory school at around the same time, but later left to join the Imperial Navy. At the battle of Tsushima, Akiyama was a staff officer under Togo Heihachiro aboard the battleship *Mikasa*, from which he sent his famous telegraph, "clear skies but high waves." Later, as a Navy captain, he was assigned as a U.S. military attaché, and around that time he visited Shiki, who by then was an invalid. He told him he was going to America, which was quite a shock for Shiki. They'd been raised under similar circumstances, yet his friend was heading off to all the countries he'd dreamed of visiting, while he himself was confined to bed. After Akiyama left, Shiki wrote a poem: "Off you go yet I remain, crying under mosquito netting." It's unclear whether his tears begrudge his friend's health or if they are an expression of sorrow for his inability to travel himself, but by that time he already had multiple ulcers on his back and no chance of recovery. Yet still his head was full of curiosity about the countries of the West.

Keene   Generally speaking, the literature of the Meiji era—its early years at the least—was quite masculine. It had a passionate spirit of building a new world, a new Japan. Which brings us back to the beginning of our conversation, in that the atmosphere of the Nara period was probably similar. But then in Shiki's period of the Meiji era things took a different twist.

Shiba   Writers started moving back to the original femininity.

Keene   Or rather, latitude for moving back developed.

Shiba   Latitude developed, eh? Now that's quite interesting.

Keene   Around that time you start seeing novels like Ozaki Koyo's *Tajo-Takon* (Passions and Regrets), which is definitely in the "feminine" genre. There's nothing masculine about it. But I think it's closely connected to a long lineage of Japanese novels. Critics go on about things like its use of colloquial language, but the most important thing about it is that it represents the first instance of Meiji-era literature actually becoming literature. Novels preceding it—for example the political novel *Kajin no Kigu* (Strange Encounters with Beautiful Women), in which Tokai Sanshi visits Independence Hall in Philadelphia—were likely interesting at the time, and without question were of a masculine bent, but when we reach *Passions and Regrets* we're finally back to a work that's in the lineage of Japanese literature.

Shiba   Yes, *Strange Encounters with Beautiful Women* is pretty much unreadable today.

Keene   Actually, I read it just recently. It's quite fun, you know. Quite fun indeed. Not to say it's well-written, but it has a uniquely innocent charm. The political novels of Sudo Nansui (1857–1920) like *Uso Manpitsu Ryokusadan* (Random Jottings by a Rainy Window) and *Ippin Issho Shinso no Kajin* (The Ladies of New Style), were published around the same time. I've been reading these books lately, and they all have this feeling of innocence. They're upbeat and optimistic, filled with themes like "imagine how wonderful it would be if Japan had a parliament," and "we can make our country a paradise on earth." But later on there's a sense of disillusionment, and we get back to the original Japanese tradition.

Shiba   I suppose so. You end up with Ito Hirobumi (1841–1909)[22] leading the charge to develop a Japanese constitution and establish the Diet before the Freedom and People's Rights Movement could explode. Doing so took the wind from the Movement's sails, while at the same time turning Japanese literature back to what it had once been.

---

22. First prime minister of Japan.

30   Chapter 1

Keene   Right. Even within the confines of the Meiji era, I think there's a qualitative difference in literature from before and after those events. Literature seems to take on a new purpose. Before, the role of literature was somewhat Confucian, it was a tool to aid in teaching the common folk. *Kajin no Kigu* is like that, as are the works by Sudo Nansui. But I feel like once the Diet was more or less established, literature stopped serving that role and went back to what it had been before. In other words, it became "feminine" literature, the literature of *mono-no-aware*[23], like that of Motoori Norinaga (1730–1801). *Tajo-Takon* is definitely a *mono-no-aware* work.

Shiba   And so we're back to where we started.

---

23. A Japanese school of literature that emphasizes wistfulness regarding the transience of all things.

CHAPTER 2

Kukai, Ikkyu, and the Universality of Religion

Shingon Buddhism as an International Religion

Shiba   I recently wrote a piece about Kukai (774–835)[1] for an anthology called *Shodo Geijutsu* (Calligraphic Art) published by Chuokoron-Sha. Honestly speaking, something about Kukai had always struck me as disagreeable. But before writing that piece, I started reading *Kukai Zenshu* (The Complete Writings of Kukai)—a very difficult work published during the Edo period—and after reading just a tenth of it or so I began to see him as actually a quite interesting person. Recently he's transformed in my mind from someone unpleasant to someone fascinating.

He left for China when he was thirty years old with a very specific goal: learning about Vajrayana, or esoteric Buddhism. He was still a student, so it's not like the government assigned him this task. He must have just up and left for his own reasons. Some small traces of esoteric Buddhism were already present in Japan, so he probably had some idea of what he was after, but it's interesting that such scant knowledge would compel him to go. He headed off to China thinking of esoteric Buddhism as the power that moves the universe, the esoteric teachings as opposed to exoteric teachings. When he reached the palace at Chang'an he did find esoteric teachings there, but they seemed a poor fit with the nature of the Chinese people. The concepts were extremely

---

1. Monk and founder of the Shingon school of Buddhism.

32   Chapter 2

theoretical. He saw all these frightening statues depicting aspects of the Buddha, which represented various concepts, but the ideas that lay beyond those Buddhas were floating out in the cosmos somewhere. The Chinese were more interested in things growing in the earth or walking on the ground, things that you could hold in your hands or eat. To the Confucian sensibility esoteric teachings were the stuff of madmen, so Vajrayana hadn't really taken root, and the great Chinese teachers of esoteric Buddhism were in something of a slump. So when Kukai showed up they gave him everything they had, and he took it back to Japan. In truth esoteric Buddhism is more a form of Brahmanism than of Buddhism. For one thing, the figure considered to be the sect's founder isn't Siddhartha Gautama but rather the mythological Vairocana Buddha, so I consider Vajrayana to be more like a local folk religion from India. But anyway, setting aside the issue of whether it's a form of Brahmanism or Indian folk religion, what had trickled into Chang'an wasn't the Buddhism of the Buddha, this brilliant individual who extracted a gem from traditional teachings, but something much more common. I don't know how deeply the monks there really understood the esoteric teachings, but that's what had been passed down for generations, and that's what Kukai received and took back to Japan.

Maybe this is a bold assertion to make, but I don't think the Shingon Buddhism that Kukai is associated with is quite the Vajrayana Buddhism he learned in Chang'an. The two are fashioned from the same stuff, but I believe Kukai did a bit of refitting, some polishing of the crystal if you will. He removed some logical flaws and built it up into the Shingon Buddhism that's practiced in the temples of Mt. Koya[2] and Toji temple. He created a perfect structure that would come toppling down if even one of its principles were removed. So his disciples

2. The mountain valley settled by Kukai that is the locus of Shingon Buddhism.

ceased further studies and Kukai came to be known by the honorific folk-name "Kobo Daishi," and Shingon Buddhism stopped developing. But that's because Kukai had perfected it to the point where no further change was needed! I find that amazing. You find Brahmanism in India because there's a need for it, and it's a living, vital thing. But you can't just bring something like that to a new land with completely different traditions. It's like Kukai was able to isolate its core components in the same way one might extract the active ingredients in Chinese herbs for use in Western medicine. I think that's why his Buddhism took root in Japan. Of course, those roots spread in an odd way, through the uneducated *Koya hijiri* monks[3] and traders who traveled throughout Japan telling people that there was this wonderful person called the Kobo Daishi, but not talking about the actual teachings of Shingon Buddhism.

Keene   That wasn't the only way esoteric Buddhism spread, though— don't forget the artwork. The Mandala of the Two Realms, for example, and images of the Acala deity, Trailokyavijaya, Vajrayaksa…

Shiba   You're right, the art did have a big influence.

Keene   I believe it was a central influence, the biggest difference between Hinayana and Mahayana Buddhism, I'd say. I visited Ceylon [Sri Lanka] a dozen or so years ago, and I got to see a temple at a very famous holy site there called Anuradhapura. It was made from stone, so it was almost unchanged from long ago, and I noticed that all the pillars were completely unadorned—just plain supports with nothing resembling artwork to be found anywhere. Well, there was just one exception, a flower motif delicately carved into the stones of a toilet. That's it. That's the Hinayana attitude towards art. But when the Kobo

---

3. Itinerant, low-caste monks sent from Mt. Koya to spread the teachings of Shingon Buddhism.

34   Chapter 2

Daishi studied with Huiguo[4], he received ceremonial items made by local sculptors, pictures of mandalas, and various other pieces of art that he brought back to Japan. He considered them *upaya*, expedient means of helping the common folk understand the teachings of Buddhism. Not only did such artwork help spread Buddhism, it also eventually developed into a wonderful art form in its own right. The Kobo Daishi is famous as a calligrapher, but even the smallest Shingon temple you visit today will have sculptures that he carved himself. It's hard to imagine something similar in any other religion.

Shiba   Shingon Buddhism expresses itself through objects, large and small. The large ones are statues of the Buddha, while the small ones include *tokko*, *sanko*, and *goko*[5]. These objects express the idea that from within the universe we can sense the breath of the cosmos. The universe is a place where the wind blows and things happen, and we can be one with that wind. When the universe exhales we experience it as wind, so it's like esoteric teachings are a way of bringing together the cosmos, its breath and digestion and such. This idea that when we become one with the cosmos we can do things such as make rain is impossible to fully explain with words, so it's represented through those ferocious Buddha images, or through chants.

Keene   I find Shingon Buddhism the most appealing of the Japanese Buddhist sects. The buildings at Mt. Koya have of course been hit by lightning and burned down many times over the years, so little of what remains is original, but if you visit today the place still has a unique, powerfully international feel to it.

---

4. The Tang-era Chinese monk at Xi Ming temple in Chang'an who passed the Vajrayana tradition on to Kukai.

5. *Ko* are traditional Indian weapons used for self-defense. Their forms were adopted as ceremonial implements representing the defeat of *kleshas*, mental states such as anger, fear, or jealousy that cloud the mind. They are metal rods with one (*tokko*), three (*sanko*), or five (*goko*) spikes on either end.

Shiba You think so? I never really noticed that.

Keene Of course I love many Japanese things, but I think religion should always be multi-cultural. All the great religions are. Mount Koya is an international place in that sense.

Shiba Now that you mention it, it does have an open feel to it.

Keene Japan imported Buddhism from the continent. That much is clear. Any book you read will say so, and no one would claim that Buddhism was born in Japan. But it's equally true that the Japanese reformed Buddhism to fit Japan to the extent possible. The Buddhism of the Kamakura period is a prime example—the teachings of Shinran (1173–1262)[6], say, or Nichiren (1222–1282)[7].

Shiba Neither Shinran nor Nichiren seem to have had much interest in the Buddha. You could even say they were happy so long as their own safety was assured, regardless of the Buddhist worldview.

Keene These are quite important matters from a cultural perspective. Still, Buddhism has always been an extremely international religion. We would be mistaken to forget that. It was shared by India, Southeast Asia, China, Mongolia... I wrote a book called *Living Japan* over a decade ago. It's not very good, I'm afraid, as I didn't yet know what I was talking about, but in that book I wrote something like, "The more one sees of Southeast Asia, the less one is able to think of Japanese Buddhism as flourishing. Compared to the countries of Southeast Asia, Buddhism in Japan is very understated." Last year I heard that this passage was used as a reading in an English textbook for Japanese students, much to the annoyance of a certain university professor. He wrote, "I take this as indicating that Buddhism is so deeply embedded

---

6. The monk who founded Jodo Shinshu Buddhism.
7. Founder of Nichiren Buddhism.

within our hearts that it can hardly be discerned by foreigners." I was quite surprised, and at the same time offended, by his statement. I thought, "What does this guy know about what I can or can't discern?"

Shiba   I had precisely the opposite experience. I don't give lectures very often, but Nara's prefectural government was insistent that I give one, so I found myself lecturing in the city of Nara. That night I said something like, "The Japanese are insensitive to principles." We'll probably touch on this again later, but one example of this would be a Japanese saying, "Dr. Keene's a foreigner, so he can't possibly understand so-and-so." Yes, Buddhism came to Japan, but as you say the countries of Southeast Asia developed through Buddhism in a more fundamental sense. In those countries, Buddhism affects *everything*, from how you live your life to the gestures you make and the way you walk. *That* is true Buddhism, and while Buddhism exists in Japan and we have some outstanding temples, it's more of an aesthetic than an actual religion or philosophy. I even went so far that night as to say Japanese Buddhism was a kind of a game played among intellectuals— only to look up and see a Buddhist nun in the audience, a woman who from all appearances had devoted her entire life to Buddhism. That certainly shut me up! I didn't want her to think I was claiming her life was without meaning.

Keene   Even so, when I recently visited Toji temple[8] for the first time, I was struck by what an impressive form of Buddhism the Shingon sect is. Actually, I'd visited ten years earlier, but the main hall wasn't open to the public at that time. On this last visit I got to go in and see the amazing Buddha statues there.

I used to think exactly as you did. When I first started learning about the Kobo Daishi and his relationship with the Dengyo Daishi[9], the

---

8. A Heian-period temple (796) in Kyoto that was for a time the residence of Kukai.

Kobo Daishi—Kukai, that is—struck me as quite disagreeable. Saicho might not have been an accomplished scholar, but he was a wonderful person in the human sense. On the other hand, Kukai was no doubt brilliant, but I found myself quite indifferent to him as a person.

Shiba   He comes across as a very nasty individual.

Keene   He does indeed. Today, however, I think he's one of the greatest geniuses in history.

Shiba   So while Saicho was smart, Kukai was a genius.

Keene   And that style he wrote in, *pianwen*, was it? Six-four…

Shiba   Four-six prose[10].

Keene   Right. The fact that he was able to use such a restricted style to so clearly express incredibly complex ideas is just magnificent, I think.

Shiba   It's also interesting that, as you mentioned before, almost every Shingon temple has objects created by the Kobo Daishi himself. That's surprising, but I suppose if you think about it, after he studied with Huiguo at Xi Ming temple it would have been quite easy for him to bring back things like sutras, but he couldn't really take large Buddha statues home. He must have brought back the plans for how to make them. When he returned to Japan he would have gathered metalworking implements and artisans, then showed pictures to the workers—you go make this, and you go make that. I wonder if that's why there are so many works by the Kobo Daishi out there.

---

9. "Dengyo Daishi" is a respectful title for Saicho (767–822), the Buddhist monk who founded the Tendai sect of Buddhism. Saicho was on the same mission to China that took Kukai there, and the two became friends. Both were instrumental in bringing esoteric Buddhism to Japan, although they later had a falling out over doctrinal issues.

10. A classical Chinese prose style that places tight restrictions on the number of characters per line, metrics, tone, etc.

38   Chapter 2

The Appeal of Ikkyu

Keene   Another person I find myself quite drawn to is Ikkyu Sojun
(1394–1481)[11]. I'd never really studied Zen Buddhism, nor had I paid
particular attention to Ikkyu, but I once saw his portrait and found it
to have such character. Normally when you see the portrait of a Zen
master you think, "What an impressive man he must have been," or
"What a stern figure," but as you know, portraits of Ikkyu have the
vividness and uniqueness of a living person to them. I started learning
about him because of those portraits, because I wanted to know more
about the kind of person he was. Of course I knew the simplified version from popular fables and the like, but I knew nothing of his Chinese poetry or of his biography. But the more I read of works like his
Kyo'unshu (Crazy Cloud Anthology)[12], the more I started to think he
was a very peculiar individual. This may sound strange, but I thought
to myself, "I really *understand* this guy." Any sense of distance I'd felt
immediately vanished, and his concerns began to feel like my own.

I first described this experience at a lecture in the United States, and
I consider that lecture one of the most successful I've ever given. There
were many young people in the audience, and all of them were moved.
Not because I'd given a skillful presentation, mind you, but because
the things that troubled Ikkyu have a certain universality and power
to move people even today. He had a fundamental hatred for hypo-
crites. He cursed them all, and while Ikkyu himself was in a sense very
selfish and lived a somewhat immoral life, I felt I could understand his
anger and indignation deep in my bones. I don't know enough about
Zen to say anything about Rinzai[13] or Dogen[14], but Ikkyu... I definitely

---

11. A well-known eccentric Zen monk who became an iconic figure in anti-authoritarian
    stories and fables, and was later popularized by the 1970s animated television show
    Ikkyu-san.
12. A collection of Chinese poetry by Ikkyu.
13. Rinzai Gigen (?–866); Chinese name: Linji Yixuan, founder of the Rinzai school of Zen
    Buddhism.

Kukai, Ikkyu, and the Universality of Religion   39

came to consider him one of the great figures in world history.

Shiba   I rather like several of the famous poems depicting his relationship with Shin, or Mori, the blind woman he took as a lover.
"Every night, Blind Mori accompanies me in song. Under the covers,
two mandarin ducks whisper to each other," and "The most beautiful and truest of all women; Her songs the fresh, pure melody of love.
A voice and sweet smile that rends my heart—I'm in a spring forest
of lovely cherry-apples."[15] There are others too, these poems where
you're amazed that he can say the things he says with such aplomb. He
would have been gutsy even by today's standards. The kindness that he
expresses for this poor blind girl, a simple temple attendant, is that of
attachment between two living beings. Not even humans—just her as a
living being, and him as a living being, and this sense in his poems that
because they're both living beings, they should be kind to each other.

Keene   Yet there's an emotional intensity in his poems that's hard to
describe. If you compare Ikkyu's poems to other Chinese poems in the
Zen Buddhist Five Mountains literature[16] it can come across as poorly
written. There are probably only two or three pages discussing Ikkyu
in the historical accounts of Five Mountains literature, and even that's
derogatory! But I don't feel a thing when I read the poetry of Gido
Shushin (1325–1388)[17]. They're pretty, I suppose, but they have nothing to do with me. That's what made reading the poems of Ikkyu such
a surprising experience—they were so easy to understand. He wrote
things like "Mori, if I ever forget my profound gratitude to you, let me
burn in hell forever,"[18] right?

---

14. Dogen Zenji (1200–1253): founder of the Soto school of Zen Buddhism.

15. Ikkyu, *Wild Ways: Zen Poems of Ikkyu*, trans. John Stevens (Boston: Shambhala, 1995)

16. Chinese-language poetry and prose composed by monks at the principle centers of
Rinzai Zen during the fourteenth and fifteenth centuries.

17. A luminary composer of the early Five Mountains tradition.

18. Ikkyu, *Wild Ways: Zen Poems of Ikkyu*, trans. John Stevens (Boston: Shambhala, 1995)

40   Chapter 2

Shiba   He did indeed.

Keene   I don't think any other Zen monk could write something like
that. There was a time when everyone was going on about Zen Buddhism overseas, and in the United States in particular. I suppose that
in an era when people were losing their faith in a Christian God, some
of them thought a godless religion might work better. Zen seemed to
fit the bill, so many people ran to that. While I'm sure some are earnest believers, for others it's more of an escape from Christianity, even
if they don't really understand the esoteric teachings of Shingon Buddhism. They appreciated the directness of a godless religion like Buddhism, but I'm not sure that what they're doing is true Zen.

Shiba   In the case of the Japanese, I suppose that of the many religions
to have come here, Zen fit our sensibilities best—setting aside the issue
of whether what's practiced here qualifies as true Zen. It just seems
to suit us. I don't know about contemporary America, but in Japan I
think a big part of Zen's appeal is its intuitiveness and lack of annoying
quibbling. For example, I sometimes wonder how the *shishi*[19] could go
happily to their deaths without even receiving funereal rites. I think,
"Did they really believe in a future? Did they really believe they would
be reincarnated?" I don't think so. I think Zen had a particular appeal
for the warriors of that time. I think some of them were satisfied simply to flicker out to nothingness. I don't know who coined the phrase
bushido, the "way of the warrior," but the definition of "warrior" var-
ies with the age. Warriors believe different things at different times, so
it's hard to pin down, but many who lived at the end of the Tokugawa
shogunate seem very Zen-like.

---

19. Anti-shogunate, anti-foreigner supporters of the emperor in the late Edo period.

The *Kirishitans*

Shiba   Perhaps it's because so many religions had already come to Japan, or perhaps it's just part of the Japanese nature, but when the Portuguese first brought Christianity—that is to say Catholicism—to Japan (1549), people don't seem to have been terribly surprised. The monks at Hieizan[20] seem to have thought at first that a new Buddhist sect had arrived.

Keene   Yes, especially at the beginning. Francis Xavier (1506–1552)[21] was unsure how to translate "God" in the European sense, and after much deliberation settled upon *"dainichi"* [literally "Great Sun" but also the name of the Vairocana Buddha.]. So when he approached the Japanese saying "We worship *dainichi*," they would just nod and think, *Ah, so these foreigners are Buddhists too.* [Laughs]

Xavier thought, "This is strange, I should be meeting with more resistance." After some research he realized dainichi was not a good translation, so he started using the Portuguese word *Deus.* I don't speak Portuguese, but I understand that his pronunciation of Deus sounded a lot like the Japanese *daiuso* ["enormous lie"]. So people would laugh at him when he went around saying, "We believe in an enormous lie." [Laughs]

Another possible explanation for the lack of alarm is that it was fortunate the Portuguese were the first to arrive. If the first foreigners to show up had been Dutch or Norwegian, the Japanese would probably have found them much stranger. If you visit Portugal today, you'll see many people who look quite Japanese. They have black hair, and their facial features aren't so far removed from the Japanese. The Japanese themselves have varied facial features, so I imagine that when they saw

---

20. The site of an influential temple complex at the time, and headquarters of the Tendai sect of Buddhism today.
21. One of the first Roman Catholic missionaries sent to Asia. He first came to Japan in 1549.

42   Chapter 2

the Portuguese, while the differences were certainly noticeable, they didn't seem like a completely different race.

Shiba   That would be particularly true for Xavier, since he was Basque, a minority group from the Pyrenees that looks especially Asian. I could definitely imagine the people of that time seeing a Basque person and thinking he looked Japanese enough.

Keene   I've read in translation many letters by Portuguese and Spanish missionaries of the time, and none of them say anything about the Japanese belonging to a different race from the Europeans. In fact, they describe Japanese women as being lighter-skinned than European women. I take this as meaning that they considered the Japanese to be basically the same kind of human being as the Europeans. Much later, with the advent of nationalism in the nineteenth century, you start to see racism appear, but at least at the time of the Portuguese arrival you don't see that. They just wrote about how nice the place was, how much cleaner than Europe. The funniest thing they write about is the vexing problem of not knowing where to spit! They would spit without hesitation in a European home, but everything in Japan was so clean it didn't seem appropriate. So while differences like that did exist, the Portuguese didn't think of the Japanese as less developed than Europeans. They only wrote about one large deficiency with Japan, namely a lack of belief in Jesus Christ. "If they can address that, Japan will be better than any European country," one wrote. Xavier even wrote that he felt closer to the Japanese than to the Portuguese. I believe those things allowed the Portuguese and Japanese to get along well. In his announcement of the Grand Kitano Tea Ceremony (1587) Toyotomi Hideyoshi said, "We welcome those from Japan of course, but also those from foreign countries who share our interests." In other words, the invitation was open to Westerners. In my experience, modern Japanese feel a certain tension when a Westerner is present. It's like they're unsure what they're doing or saying is appropriate in the presence of a Westerner, or perhaps that they might be subjected to uncomfortable topics of conversation. But it seems like the Japanese of that earlier time didn't feel that way at all.

Shiba   Westerners were welcomed, in fact. There were, what, half a million Catholics in Japan at one point? Catholicism was spreading like wildfire. There has to be something beyond the universality of religion behind that. Part of it was probably that people were growing tired of Japanese Buddhism, and maybe, as you suggested, some saw Catholicism as another branch of Buddhism. But certainly the major factor was that, as you just mentioned, the people and institutions of other nations weren't seen as being objectionable.

Take, for example, the famous story of Hosokawa Gracia (1563–1600)[22] and her husband, Tadaoki (1563–1645)[23]. They were a close couple with very old-fashioned habits—the very picture of a medieval couple with all the requisite passions and whatnot, but very close from what I understand. Not just in the normal sense, but also as partners in philosophical debates. Gracia became interested in Zen Buddhism when she was fourteen or fifteen, and would go to visit Zen monks and read Confucian works. Tadaoki made quite an effort to be of service to his beautiful bride, by which I mean he would visit monks to learn about philosophical subjects like the structure of the universe and the secrets of life, then relate to Gracia what he had learned. He did this because he knew it made Gracia happy. Then one day he came back with stories about the Portuguese—"They have this thing called God ..."

---

22. Born Akechi Tama, she was the daughter of Akechi Mitsuhide, who was famous for leading the rebellion against Oda Nobunaga in which Nobunaga was killed.

23. A samurai originally in service to Oda Nobunaga and later the lord of Kokura, in modern-day Fukuoka prefecture.

44   Chapter 2

In the end Gracia converted to Catholicism, though her husband did not. This was Akechi Mitsuhide's daughter, so she lived a turbulent life, one that ended in tragedy at the Battle of Sekigahara[24]. After the fighting was over Tadaoki returned to Osaka, where the couple had maintained a mansion in Tamazukuri. There was a church nearby that had always been a sore point for Tadaoki—Gracia had formed close connections there and frequently visited in secret despite her husband's pleas that she stay away—but Tadaoki gave a donation to the priest there. A very large donation, which the priest turned around and used for local orphans and the poor. The entire donation was immediately used up in this way, surprising Tadaoki to no end. Japanese monks of course took in donations as well, but they never used the money that way, so Tadaoki was deeply moved. Nevertheless he was a politician, and the government at the time was moving toward forbidding Christianity, which meant there was no chance of him converting, but I can't help but wonder if he didn't want to for the rest of his life. Partly in remembrance of his wife, but also because that priest had used the money he'd donated after his wife's death for the less fortunate. Tadaoki seems to have been truly touched by that.

Anyway, stories like that make me think that up until the end of Japan's Warring States period—or at least up to the time in the early Tokugawa shogunate when expulsion of Catholics began in earnest—the Japanese were much more accommodating of foreigners.

Keene   I'm currently writing a series of books called *A History of Japanese Literature*, and as part of that I've recently been reading about the Edo-period haiku poet Matsunaga Teitoku (1571–1653). I can't think of a more conservative poet, or one with less concern for religious and cultural freedom, yet he visited churches without inhibition

---

24. A famous battle in 1600 that was the first step toward Tokugawa Ieyasu establishing his shogunate.

and had relationships with several Christians. In one of his letters he wrote that he'd recently acquired a cask of delicious foreign wine from Nagasaki and invited a friend to come drink it with him. It's hard to imagine something like that happening at the height of the Tokugawa shogunate!

CHAPTER 3

The World of Gold, the World of Silver: The Aesthetics of Troubled Times

Ashikaga Yoshimasa and Higashiyama Culture

Shiba   Japanese culture is often said to have come into its own during the Heian period (794–1180), but the culture our daily lives revolve around today—things like architecture and philosophy—actually originated mostly in the Muromachi period (1337–1573). That's when the Japanese tea ceremony and ikebana flower arrangement developed, as well as *noh* theater and *kyogen*[1], and the first forms of Japanese dance worth watching. From what I understand, the Japanese proclivity for keeping records of everything also emerged in the late Muromachi period, even among commoners and uneducated samurai. I'm not sure what caused these developments, but that's what seems to have happened. I wonder, too, if the language of kyogen didn't become the standard Japanese dialect of the time and eventually evolve into the Japanese we speak today. The language used in the noh and kyogen of Kyoto or wherever it was spread to the furthermost borders of Tsugaru[2] in the north and Tanegashima[3] in the south, and in some cases even as far as Okinawa. So perhaps the language of noh and its

---

1. A traditional form of Japanese comic theater often performed as interludes during more serious noh plays.
2. In present-day Aomori prefecture, at the northern tip of the main Japanese island, Honshu.
3. An island off the southern coast of Kyushu, part of present-day Kagoshima prefecture.

48   Chapter 3

choral lyrics inadvertently pushed the Japanese language toward stan-
dardization, and once a standard language was established, it became
easier to keep records. Starting in the late Muromachi period and
continuing through the Warring States era, anonymous authors left
behind many records telling about their experiences in wars. I wonder
if it wasn't the language they heard in entertainment, this drama that
developed in Kyoto and spread throughout Japan, that allowed them to
keep these records describing how they went to war and what they saw
there. That's just my pet theory, mind you.

Keene   I used to take a particular interest in medieval Japan and the
Muromachi period, and in Higashiyama culture in particular. Even so,
I've always felt puzzled by Ashikaga Yoshimasa (1436–1490), who one
might call its central figure. He's always been a complete mystery to
me. You can see a statue of him if you visit Ginkakuji temple[4], but even
looking at the face it's difficult to draw any conclusions. Was this an
extremely honorable man? A terribly violent man? It's hard to imagine. To my knowledge no Japanese scholar has ever written a detailed
biography of him, and he's not even listed in the latest edition of the
Jinbutsu Sosho (Historical Monographs). I assume this is due to insuf-
ficient source material, but I wish someone would at least compile what
scholarly knowledge does exist.

I can't imagine what his life must have been like while he was still at
Hana no gosho[5], before he built the Ginkaku villa. The fiercest battles
of the Onin War[6] were fought within sight of the place. Nevertheless,
Yoshimasa went on having love affairs and hosting drunken banquets.
The legends we've all heard of the Roman emperor Nero playing a

4. Also called "the Temple of the Silver Pavilion," built in Kyoto as Yoshimasa's retirement
villa and converted to a Rinzai Zen temple after his death.
5. "The Flower Palace," the Kyoto residence of the Ashikaga clan.
6. A civil war (1467–1477) that initiated the Warring States period, fought over who would
inherit the shogunate when Yoshimasa died or retired.

fiddle as he watched Rome burn are almost certainly fabricated, but in Yoshimasa's case, the truth is he continued his stylish pursuits at Hana no gosho even as people died in the streets around him. Something like nine-tenths of Kyoto burned during the Onin War. It is well-summed up by a tanka poem[7] of the time: "Oh evening skylarks over the ruins of my capital! / Do you see how my teardrops fall as I watch you soar?" It's difficult to even imagine such a scene.

Shiba   Yes, you're probably right that Yoshimasa's worldview is hard for people like us to fathom. Many scholars are interested in Yoshimasa, but as you say, clear information and biographies are lacking. The historians Nakamura Naokatsu and Tsuji Zennosuke did a bit of research, as did the literary critic Karaki Junzo, but none of them wrote specifically about Yoshimasa. The Muromachi era reached its zenith during Yoshimasa's Higashiyama period—certainly more so than during the Kitayama period of [his grandfather] Ashikaga Yoshimitsu (1358–1408). Yoshimasa saw the Onin War raging and people starving and dying right before his eyes, but he continued drinking and building his beautiful pavilion. It's hard to understand how a person could be so callous.

And yet he appears to have been quite kind to the people he knew, and not just the nobility. Take for example the *ami* class. Of course in Yoshimasa's era the extreme class-based discrimination of the Edo period didn't yet exist, but even so, farmers who didn't own rice paddies—including those with only dry fields—were looked down on. The dryland farmers were lower on the social scale than the rice farmers, and those with no land at all were even further down. Those folks at the bottom congregated along riverbanks and other places that didn't really belong to anyone, and scraped by growing daikon and such. Many of them became gardeners or performers or peddlers, but when

---

7. By Inoo Tsunefusa (1422–1485).

these so-called "riverbank people" visited other people's homes they wouldn't normally be invited inside as guests. Yet Yoshimasa did invite them in, and almost treated them as equals—though that's probably not quite the right phrase to use. In any case, he's the only shogun to have ever said that all people are equal. Of all the pre-Meiji nobles, only Yoshimasa said that humans are humans, you as much as any shogun. Still, he did nothing in the political sphere, even as he watched the Onin War unfold. He seems to have completely given up on any kind of political solution. Legally he was the protector of the people, but he completely avoided politics. The daimyo below him were powerful, ignorant, and greedy. They didn't practice politics so much as scheme against each other, so it's no wonder he did everything he could to avoid getting involved. I wonder if he wasn't trying to create a world he could escape into.

Keene   Yet Yoshimasa knew his people were starving, and still he spent almost nothing on them, even as he rebuilt the Hana no gosho palace. And he was happy to spend money on things that would entertain him. Sure, he was an important patron of the arts, and gave plenty of money to artists, but people were starving to death all around him. No matter how much you hate politics, if you consider others to be fellow human beings it seems like you would also consider their death to somehow be connected with yourself.

Shiba   I suppose his feelings about human equality weren't something he felt deep in his bones. They were more like simple notions or ideas. His continuing to say that all people are equal was his ideal, and putting that into practice would have meant feeding the starving, but he lived on ideas, not actions. As a human being myself I don't want there to be people like that, but I guess Yoshimasa was an example of living solely in the world of ideals.

Actually, today is the first time I've seen the Ginkakuji temple pavilion. I came once before long ago, but I got in a huge fight with some monks at the gate who annoyed me by peddling their souvenirs so persistently, so I left. But I'm glad I got my first look tonight, with this lovely crescent moon and the good weather you've brought with you—you seem to have chased away all the clouds from earlier today. The Silver Pavilion under this soft moonlight is like a perfect expression of beauty. It almost seems like it couldn't have been made by human hands alone, like something beyond mortal flesh must have been involved. You said something when we saw the wooden statue of Yoshimasa at, where, the Togu Hall, was it? You mentioned that he looks like a normal person. He doesn't have a heroic countenance, or the serene atmosphere of one seeking enlightenment—he just looks like someone you might bump into on the street. I guess we should be careful how much we read into a statue, but you get this feeling of "Huh, so this is the famous Hino Tomiko's husband."[8] Yoshimasa seems to have had a strange relationship with Tomiko. They became estranged and she went off and made a lot of money by questionable means, which he then turned around and borrowed to build this world for himself... So I suppose he was probably just a man dedicated to that—to creating his own world. Of course when you look at his reputation as a politician he's absolutely awful.

Keene   Today Ginkakuji is of course a famous Zen temple, but although Yoshimasa did follow Zen, he was also a believer in Jodo Buddhism, and various superstitions as well.

Shiba   Yes, the Togu Hall was dedicated to the Amitabha Buddha of Jodo , which wouldn't be necessary for someone seeking enlightenment through Zen. Jodo is for those who want the Buddha to come greet them upon their death, those who are in the East but seek to be

---

8. Tomiko sought the help of other daimyo to support her son's claim as heir to the shogunate, thus instigating the Onin War.

52   Chapter 3

reborn in the West[9]. How very like Yoshimasa, to want to be reborn in paradise! None of that is needed if you've attained enlightenment, so this makes Yoshimasa an all the more dubious character.

Keene   Everything about the Higashiyama period is interesting. Every book I've read about the Onin War and what happened before and after it has been interesting to me, but something about Yoshimasa, its central character, remains hazy. I just can't understand him, not deeply. I suspect he might have been a touch insane.

Shiba   In some sense he must have been. He seems to have been incapable of viewing reality as truly real.

The Onin War as Revolution

Keene   I'd like to consider the "silver" in the Silver Pavilion for a bit. To the Japanese at the time, gold was surely more valuable and precious than silver. Yoshimitsu had already built the Golden Pavilion, so Yoshimasa knew from the outset that his building would be less grand. Not only was silver less precious then gold, but also if you compare the buildings themselves, the Golden Pavilion is a much more impressive piece of architecture. So I wonder if Yoshimasa wasn't aware from the start of the limits to the world he could create.

Shiba   Or he may have intentionally created those limits.

Keene   Right, expressing that he lived in a silver era, not a golden one. Now this is just my own idea, but considering the tastes of the Japanese I wonder if silver isn't better suited to them than gold. To me, the somehow forlorn feeling of silver seems more Japanese than the warm yellow glow of gold. Zeami (1363–1443)[10] wrote in his essay *Kyui* (The

---

9. A reference to the Platform Sutra.
10. A famous noh actor during the Muromachi period.

Nine Levels) that various levels of flower exist, and one of these has the beauty of a silver bowl collecting snow. To me, that is an extremely Japanese sense of beauty. Perhaps in that sense the Japanese were able to feel closer to the Silver Pavilion than the Golden one. Other artifacts of Higashiyama also feel as if they come from a world of silver— the monochromatic *sumi-e* paintings, for instance, and the flower arrangement and tea ceremony. Of course, all kinds of tastes exist within Japan, but if I were forced to narrow them down to one specific aesthetic to represent this country, I'd have to say it's that of Higashiyama Culture.

Shiba   I would have to agree.

Keene   Now there *are* examples of exquisitely gorgeous artwork, like the *Tale of Genji Scroll* and some paintings, but only a few. On the other hand, countless excellent pieces in the lineage of Higashiyama culture and the Silver Pavilion exist. I think it's because they feel more familiar to the Japanese, or easier to understand.

Shiba   Yes, I think most Japanese would find the Golden Pavilion to be a bit garish and the Silver Pavilion more subdued in the sense of the comparison you just made between gold and silver, not necessarily as one's impression upon visiting them.

Keene   I suppose one person who represents Higashiyama culture would be Sogi (1421–1502).

Shiba   Oh yes, he's highly representative.

Keene   Sogi is known as a traveling poet, and I've read that when he was invited to distant lands, he was given a more lavish reception than even a visiting daimyo. I don't think that could have happened in an earlier era. This was toward the beginning of the Muromachi period. Considering that even Yoshida Kenko (1283?–1352)[11] was belittled in

54   Chapter 3

his time, I don't think someone like Sogi could have come to prominence any earlier.

Shiba   Kenko lived at the dawn of the Muromachi period, and his
parents were public officials, so he came from a respected family.
Even so, nobody paid attention to him. By Sogi's time the Muromachi
period was reaching maturity, and artists and intellectuals were much
more respected, so he would have been treated very differently. If you
were a countryside daimyo and someone like Sogi neglected to visit
you it would be a terrible loss of prestige, so you would do everything
possible to have your invitation accepted.

Keene   Many nobles fled to the countryside as a result of the Onin
War. I think that led to an abrupt flourishing of culture in rural areas.

Shiba   It was quite sudden, yes.

Keene   That's why you see gardens and paintings by Sesshu (1420–
1506)[12] all over the place. Had he been born a little earlier, you'd probably only see his works in Kyoto.

Shiba   Looking back on the Onin War from a later age, it seems
meaningless, almost frivolous, but I do think it changed the course of
Japanese history. For one thing, all these no-name *ashigaru* infantry-
men were running about doing the fighting in place of the samurai,
who apparently were afraid they might actually get hurt. After a while,
the ashigaru began to realize how power worked in their world, and
they started to make fun of the samurai. All kinds of authority existed
in medieval Japan—the religious authority of the temples, the authority of the noble houses, the authority of the Muromachi daimyo, and
the authority of bloodlines. Power was built up through a combination

---

11. A Buddhist monk best known for writing *Tsurezuregusa* (Essays in Idleness).
12. A famous sumi-e painter of the mid-Muromachi period.

The World of Gold, the World of Silver: The Aesthetics of Troubled Times   55

of these, but in the Higashiyama period that whole system started to fade away into a ghost of what it once was. I think the Onin War was the last straw. After that, notable figures start rising from the ranks of commoners, to the extent that following the long tenure of the Oda clan[13] during the Warring States period, their former retainers the Tokugawa[14] took control. Tokugawa Ieyasu and his family were originally farmers and woodcutters, though in the early Edo period they fabricated an impressive lineage. In fact, most of the Edo-period warrior nobles came from commoner stock, which I think is a direct result of the disruptions of the Onin War.

The Onin War was odd in that it wasn't about revolution, or even really about winning or losing, but when we view it through a modern lens it looks a lot like an organic revolution. It lacked genuine leaders and revolutionary ideals, but taking an ecological view of history, it had the effects of a revolution. From a cultural perspective too, the war had the effect of popularizing tastes that had developed primarily in Kyoto, such as adding *tokonoma* alcoves to rooms and using cedar in construction because of its odd shapes. So perhaps the more interesting point isn't so much what kind of person Yoshimasa was, but rather the long-term historical effects of all these people crazily running about during the Onin War.

Keene   Following that line of thought, maybe it's a good thing the library of regent Ichijo Kaneyoshi (1402–1481) burned during the Onin War. Most Japan scholars today believe that the burning of that library resulted in the loss of many precious stories and collections of poetry, but if all that Heian-era knowledge had remained, it might have prevented the birth of the new culture that followed.

---

13. One of the most prominent daimyo families involved in the unification of Japan. Oda Nobunaga was a particularly influential figure.

14. Starting with Tokugawa Ieyasu, this family led the Tokugawa shogunate, which ruled Japan from 1600 until the Meiji Restoration in 1868.

56   Chapter 3

Shiba   Well now there's an interesting thought indeed!

The Revival of Gold–The Azuchi–Momoyama Period

Shiba   Going back to our earlier discussion of Japan's preference
for silver versus gold, the period when Ashikaga Yoshimitsu built the
Golden Pavilion was an era of extensive trade with East Asia. Various
trading ports similar to modern-day Hong Kong were developing along
the Chinese coast south of the Yangtze river, and merchants from
those towns would visit Japan. Japanese merchants went to China,
too. Ashikaga Yoshimitsu wanted to get in on that and make some
money. The Ashikaga shogunate was a relatively poor ruling family,
you see, so they were rather obsessed with bringing in cash. Because
the lands around them were already controlled by powerful daimyo,
they sent trading ships to Ming China. Yoshimitsu took full advantage
of the fact that trade in East Asia was flourishing, and eventually his
coffers were overflowing with gold. Of course, it was the merchants of
Kyoto who did the actual money-making. Yoshimitsu's trade policy
was designed largely for the benefit of the Ashikaga clan, since they
got to make the rules, but it was implemented by commoners who
went out and traded goods. These folk were extremely low on the social
spectrum—much lower than Kenko, who we talked about earlier,
and more along the lines of Sogi—but they became something like
friends with Yoshimitsu. They'd make deals with him, saying that in
exchange for half the profits they'd go out and do the trading. Ashikaga
Yoshimasa wasn't able to carry on international trade in the same
way, though. It wasn't the *sakoku* era, when foreign trade was tightly
regulated, but situations overseas created barriers to trade for one reason or another, and it was behind these barriers that Higashiyama
culture developed. This was the era during which, as you said, charac-
teristic "Japanese" culture arose—Yoshimasa's silver era, as opposed to

Yoshimitsu's golden era.

But much later, when Oda Nobunaga (1534–1582) controlled Kyoto, gold enjoyed a glittering comeback. Nobunaga commissioned many *rakuchu rakugai* screen paintings[15], which were his idea. If he were alive today he might have been an artist. He probably only ended up a warrior because of the era he was born is.

Nobunaga had a problem, namely Uesugi Kenshin (1530–1578) of Echigo province, whose army was too powerful to defeat. Since Nobunaga couldn't beat Kenshin on the battlefield, he tricked him instead. He sent diplomats with a message saying, "It seems you wish to take Kyoto and rule all of Japan. I'll meet you at the Karahashi bridge[16] and back you up. I'll be your vanguard into Kyoto." Kenshin fell for it. To seal the deal, Nobunaga sent one of these painted screens as a gift, to show what a wonderful place Kyoto was. That screen, which today is kept at the Count Uesugi Residence, was the first one commissioned by Nobunaga. It was painted by Kano Eitoku (1543–1590)[17] and became a template for many similar paintings up through the early Edo period. When daimyos came to pay homage to Toyotomi Hideyoshi or the other shoguns, they would be given a screen painted by Kano or another artist to take back as a souvenir of Kyoto. The paintings were done in exaggerated palettes with plenty of gold, and always included the figure of a Portuguese or other foreigner—that was vital. Or they'd show some non-Japanese breed of dog walking along. They always had to be walking. Or in some cases there would be a figure who appeared to be African, brought along as an attendant to the foreigners. Nobunaga wanted to show what a cosmopolitan place Kyoto was, with foreigners coming to visit and all.

---

15. Folding screens painted with elaborate scenes of Kyoto and the surrounding areas, characterized by extensive use of gold leaf.
16. A bridge over the Seta river in modern-day Shiga prefecture, and at the time a vital strategic point for anyone invading Kyoto.
17. Founder of the Kano school of Japanese painting.

58   Chapter 3

I had one of these screens at my home for a time. It looked like it had just been painted yesterday, and I had a wonderful time poring over it with a magnifying glass. There were foreigners all over the place. The Kyoto National Museum once had an exhibition of these screens, and I believe mine was included. The museum was keeping it, at least, so I assume they showed it. I wasn't able to attend the exhibit, but I did get to look at a catalog of all the screens that were exhibited. There were foreigners in every one.

Anyway, to get back to the discussion of glittery gold versus more subdued silver, in that sense Ashikaga Yoshimasa may have created a uniquely Japanese aesthetic. That may even be why the Higashiyama period developed. But Japan later on expanded its horizons even further, not just to China but to the Western nations. The era starting with Oda and Toyotomi (the Azuchi–Momoyama Period) and extending through the early Tokugawa period was like Japan's second youth, with the introduction of Christianity we discussed before, and all kinds of new things. The rakuchu rakugai screen paintings represent this new youth of Japanese culture. The Higashiyama period was a more understated silver age, and that austerity is fine. But even so you later see gold used extensively. For instance, screens painted for castles often had a golden background with a large pine tree on it. One theory is that these were so common because the painters got really busy. New castles were popping up all over the place, and if artists painted something with too much detail they wouldn't be able to keep up. So artists like Kano had studios where they could use huge, broom-like brushes to sketch out images, then hand them over to apprentices to color in. These became the gorgeous, almost overdone works that I think represent a revival of Japanese interest in gold. Just like in Ashikaga Yoshimitsu's time, people were throwing open a window to the world, and gold was the color that represented that feeling. When that window closed again, something more "Japanese" developed—the return of silver. The same cycle repeats itself throughout the history of Japanese culture.

The Japanese Sense of Beauty

Keene   It's hard to pin down exactly what is "Japanese," what is truly unique to Japan. For example, if someone asked me what kind of pottery was distinctly Japanese, I'd probably say the same thing as pretty much anyone else—that Shino ware and Oribe ware are the most Japanese, as opposed to something like Kakiemon ware. Pottery that appears less refined, in other words, though of course a lot of skill goes into achieving that unrefined look. I think that's more Japanese than elegant Imari or Kakiemon porcelain. Now in China or Korea, if you had something with exactly the same rough style, I don't think it would be considered artistic.

Shiba   It wouldn't have been viewed as something of high quality in those places, in other words.

Keene   I think they'd see it as something farmers would use or something poorly crafted. But the Japanese put a lot of effort into that rough look. Of course it goes without saying that I've been highly influenced by Japan, to the point where it's hard for me to look at Japanese things with the fresh eyes of a foreigner. But when I see objects like that, I feel like they're very Japanese. What's hard to explain is why I feel that way about them, but not about porcelain made in Japan.

Shiba   I know what you mean, though. Think of Sen no Rikyu (1522–1591)[18] holding up a rustic tea bowl and claiming it's worth a mountain of gold. Rikyu never painted a picture or constructed a building, never really created anything as an artist, but he was an artist nonetheless, in the sense that he could find beauty in a teacup discarded by the

---

18. One of the foremost developers of the Japanese tea ceremony, notable for his emphasis on simple settings and unadorned implements.

60   Chapter 3

side of the road. But simply appreciating that beauty wasn't enough for Furuta Oribe (1544–1615)[19]—he smashed a perfectly good teacup, then glued the pieces back together using a mixture of gold and lacquer. The resulting seams formed a natural branching pattern that pleased Oribe with its coloration and weight. Finding beauty in something that's been broken and put back together is yet another level of aesthetic sensibility. But for Oribe it wasn't simply something broken, it was something he broke himself and "created" by putting back together.

Keene   Yes, I don't think that's something you see in Western culture. In Europe, for example, if you had a painting by Rembrandt that had been preserved so well for generations that it looked just the same as when Rembrandt painted it, well, that would be considered quite a treasure. Time isn't a desired factor, you see. It would be the fact that the colors were just as vivid today as on the day it was painted, as if no time had passed at all, that would please everyone so much. But I remember hearing in a lecture about Arabian aesthetics that this isn't the case for Arabs. They want to feel the era in which a thing was made. I don't speak Arabic, but I do know the word *baraka*, which is related to the English word "baroque." It means "treasure." As I understand it, it's a value that increases with age, although it's a mystical term that's difficult to define. Baraka wouldn't be present in a Rembrandt that looked today just as it did when it was created. You would only feel baraka in something that showed its age, such as a painting that had clearly survived for three hundred years, cracks and all. I think that's quite similar to the spirit of Rikyu.

Shiba   Very similar indeed. And not just Rikyu. Take the statue of the Maitreya Bodhisattva at Koryuji temple in Uzumasa, Kyoto. We look at it now and consider it a beautiful piece, but when it was created

---

19. A student of Rikyu, and founder of the Oribe school of tea ceremony.

it was probably a gaudy thing covered in gold leaf. It probably also had some kind of decoration on its head. I don't think that would be quite so attractive to us today. We prefer it with its gilding and original paint stripped down to bare wood, and that wood darkened over the past millennium or so. We find that more interesting, and more beautiful. I think people in China would prefer to repaint it. They definitely would in Korea. You've seen how the vermilion on old buildings like the Horyuji temple is peeling away, but if that temple were in Korea, it would have been repainted time and again. Moreover, they prefer to do so in brilliant blues and reds, like the Toshogu shrine in Nikko.

Keene   It's interesting that you bring up the Toshogu shrine, since it's so gaudily decorated. I understand that the Japanese used to say—and maybe still do say—that you can't call another building beautiful until you've seen Toshogu shrine. I wonder what that means?

Shiba   Well, it's beyond me. I find Nikko to be rather vulgar. It was built around the same time as the Katsura imperial villa, right? It's almost hard to believe that the two are contemporaries. I can't stand the place. Actually, I'd avoided Nikko for a long time, but I've seen it from above, from a helicopter. I wanted to see the Ueno area of Tokyo from the sky, so I flew around Ueno's Kan'eiji temple. From above, it's easy to see how big the temple grounds used to be. Nowadays there's a library and a museum and an art school and all this stuff, but from above you can see the full extent of what used to be Kan'eiji temple. You can also see that the area now covered with Ueno Station train tracks used to be a cliff. You can see all that in five minutes, and since I still had some charter time left the pilot asked if there was anywhere else I wanted to go. I'd never seen Nikko, so I asked him to take me there. We headed off to the area, which was cloudy despite Tokyo having fine weather. I asked him to show me the Yomei gate, and he descended just low enough to make it out. So I've only seen it from the sky, but it was

62   Chapter 3

just as ugly as I'd expected.

Keene   What a relief. [Laughs] I first visited Nikko just after the war, in December 1945, I believe. I remember it was snowing. I'm pretty sure nobody had kept the place up during the war, but there was the snow, and no tourists aside from myself, so it was quite nice.

Shiba   The villa at Katsura was built by Prince Hachijo Toshihito (1579–1629)[20], who was somewhat marginalized due to the circumstances of the time, but the Toshogu shrine was built in the third generation after the Tokugawa clan had established nationwide control. It was a memorial to Ieyasu, who'd unified Japan for the first time, and daimyos from all over the country contributed to the project. In other words, it's the ultimate symbol of Japanese sycophancy to authority in that era, and I wonder if that isn't why it's so gaudy—to show that the daimyos were groveling as best they could. The goal wasn't to build the most beautiful place possible, but the most decorated, as a display of adulation. Or perhaps it was meant to be a tribute to that golden age, the Azuchi–Momoyama period. That was a very open time, and as we discussed earlier, gold was representative of its mood. The Tokugawa period was more closed, but perhaps people were mimicking the resplendence of the past. In any case, it may be due to the ugliness of imitation, but if you only showed someone Nikko, I think they'd be misled regarding the aesthetic sense of the Japanese.

---

20. Younger brother of Emperor Go-Yozei.

CHAPTER 4
The Japanese View of War

Fidelity and Betrayal

Keene　There's something I've been meaning to ask you about. Reading about Japanese history, you see all of these battles taking place between the Genpei War (1180–1185) and the Warring States period (c. 1467–c. 1603), and in so many of them victory seems to have come through betrayal. In China you read about one side or the other using the strategies of Sun Tzu in its attacks, and so winning through martial skill, but in Japan a traitor always seems to appear at some decisive moment to determine the outcome of battle. It happened at the battle of Dan-no-ura[1], the battle of Sekigahara[2]... I have trouble understanding this Japanese approach to victory. What should I make of it? I mean, these are historical events that can't be ignored. Is there some meaning behind this kind of behavior?

Shiba　You're right, a traitor always does seem to appear right at the peak of battle. Not only that, but they aren't considered traitors until much later in history. In the case of Dan-no-ura, warriors from what's now Oita prefecture—the Ogata clan—first allied themselves with the Taira clan, but flipped to the Minamoto side during the battle, giving the Minamoto an advantage in the number of ships they could deploy. And as you say, a traitor determined the outcome of the battle

---

1. A decisive naval engagement in the Genpei War.
2. The battle that led to Tokugawa Ieyasu establishing the Tokugawa shogunate.

64   Chapter 4

at Sekigahara as well.

I think this happened because Japanese society was so tightly interwoven, with relatives and connections on all sides. Even when two factions were facing one another as enemies, the reason for the conflict wasn't always clear. There weren't stark distinctions like you see in Europe, where people would use religion, for example, and say things like "They're Catholics and we're Protestants." Well, I guess there were the *ikko-ikki* uprisings[3], but that's not quite what we're talking about here. Anyway, you'd have one group of related people over here fighting with another group of relatives over there, and as the conflict heated up, a point would come where it would be more beneficial to someone on one side or the other to just tear the whole thing down from the inside, and the other side would take advantage of that. Because everyone is playing on the same board, right? You even see this quite recently, for instance with the left-wing radicals in the early Showa period (1926–1989). A detective would be questioning a radical youth or a member of the Communist Party, and as they talked they'd find out they went to the same high school or something, bringing them closer and knocking down the barriers that separated them. Oddly enough, something similar happened during many of Japan's wars.

Look at the battle of Waterloo. The British army won by allying with the Prussians, and the fate of the battle rested on if, when, and where those allies would show up. In the end they did show up, and Napoleon was defeated. All cut and dried, right? No betrayals or anything, just battlefield tactics involving a hidden Wellington ally.

From a historical perspective, the battle of Sekigahara was as important as Waterloo, so you might expect the two sides to just have at it, but instead there's this ebb and flow, with the Western Army winning in the

---

3. Fifteenth- and sixteenth-century uprisings against samurai rule by peasant and clergy followers of Jodo Shinshu Buddhism.

morning and the Eastern Army winning in the afternoon, and some betrayal in-between. But the actual fighting isn't all that interesting to the Japanese—it's just a bit of drama. What's really interesting is what's going on behind the scenes. Hideyoshi's widow is whispering into Kobayakawa Hideaki's (1577–1602)[4] ear, urging him to flip to the Eastern side and support the Tokugawas. But when the actual battle rolls around, the Western Army appears poised for victory, so Kobayakawa is sitting there unsure of what to do. Tokugawa Ieyasu sends a fearsome envoy to get him moving, saying, "You said you were going to join our side. Well are you, or aren't you?" and Hideaki becomes this reluctant traitor. So the war itself is almost incidental to the story—it's the playing out of something that's already been decided. All the real drama took place back in the dressing rooms.

I tend to bring this up a lot, so it's a little embarrassing to mention it again, but around 1884 a staff officer of the Prussian Army named Major Jakob Meckel—the prize pupil of Field Marshal Helmuth von Moltke—was invited to Japan to help create a German-style general staff office for the Imperial Japanese Army. One day he visited the site of the battle of Sekigahara for some on-site lessons. After Meckel heard an overview of how the various forces were arranged on the field, he said, "So Ishida[5] won, right?" [Laughs] Of course, Meckel knew nothing of Japanese history, so when he was told that Ishida lost, he couldn't believe it. "He must have won," Meckel said. "With his forces deployed like that, how could he lose?" It was only when the betrayal was described to him that he finally relented and admitted that loss was possible in such a situation. But that's the kind of backstage drama that's most important to the Japanese, all of that maneuvering before the actual event.

---

4. Nephew of Toyotomi Hideyoshi and initially a general in the Western Army at the battle of Sekigahara.
5. Ishida Mitsunari (1559–1600), commander of the Western Army under Toyotomi Hideyoshi.

66   Chapter 4

What's difficult for the Japanese to understand is the French Revolution. During that revolution Robespierre made a speech, and immediately afterwards the mob rushed off to haul the nobility to the guillotine. Now *that* I find amazing—that his words could carry such weight. In Japan, words are just a facet of etiquette. They don't necessarily reflect what a person really thinks. This is one reason the Japanese are so bad at making speeches. When the Liberal Democratic Party conducts a general assembly of the Japanese Diet, it's simply a performance of decisions taken at meetings the night before. Like the battle of Sekigahara, it's an act, with all the drama taking place during the backstage preparations. There's nothing dramatic about war, either. It's all just a show, like an exposition—not something like the Olympics, where winners and losers are determined at the actual event. So yes, the drama of Japanese society all occurs in the background.

Keene   I guess that would be less surprising if Japan lacked a concept of loyalty, but what's odd is that so much betrayal happens in a society that goes on and on about the importance of loyalty.

Shiba   Well, loyalty does exist, but it's in the master–servant relationships where one party directly recompenses the other. For example, the Tokugawa shogunate had a formal agreement with their vassals, the Shimazu clan of Satsuma[6], but the average person back then wouldn't have seen it that way. They would have seen the Shimazu as affiliates of the Tokugawa, similar to a subsidiary company today. A subsidiary isn't necessarily "loyal" to its parent company, and in the end, when the situation called for it, the Shimazu did help bring down the Tokugawa shogunate. But a samurai of Satsuma would have been loyal to the lord of the Shimazu clan—although with a complex kind of loyalty that's hard to spell out exactly.

---

6. Modern-day western Kagoshima prefecture.

For example, the samurai of Kamakura[7] all had entourages. Say a samurai—we'll call him Kaneko—had thirty hired farmhands under him that he considered his entourage. Then Kaneko became affiliated under some other guy called Kumagai, who in turn was under Minamoto no Yoritomo (1147–1199)[8]. Kaneko's thirty farmhands—in other words the men he'd take to war if necessary—would have been loyal to him, but not to Yoritomo, and probably not to the guy one level down, either, to Kumagai. So loyalty at the time was something that only extended within arm's reach, almost like the loyalty of a dog. A dog might be loyal to the hand that feeds it, or even to the master of the house, but it barks at everyone else. I think that was pretty much the model of loyalty among the Kamakura samurai. Ideas of loyalty took on a stricter, more Confucian slant in the Edo period, but during the Warring States period it's hard to find examples of what we'd call loyalty today. The loyalty that did exist was pretty fleeting, and makes more sense when viewed as a self-serving strategy, or as a way to present yourself as a great guy.

Keene   That reminds me that the soldiers in Renaissance Italy were actually mostly mercenaries, largely Swiss. Switzerland was a very poor country at the time, and many of the men there were happy to become mercenaries since they had no better options. They didn't have any desire to fight for Switzerland, though.

Shiba   A lot of Swiss mercenaries fought for the royals in the French Revolution, too. I'm pretty amazed at how well they fought, given that they were hired men.

Keene   I'd say that's a Swiss virtue. [Laughs]

---

7. The de facto capital of Japan during the Kamakura shogunate (1192–1333), located in modern-day southern Kanagawa prefecture.
8. First shogun of the Kamakura shogunate.

68   Chapter 4

Prisoners of War

Keene   Speaking from my own experiences during World War II, I found that Japanese soldiers in that war considered being taken prisoner an absolute sin. They were told, "Never live to experience shame as a prisoner,"[9] so they treated being taken prisoner as shameful, even if they'd been captured because they were knocked unconscious by a bomb or something like that. They seemed to feel very strongly that they had let down their country. Many of them demanded to be killed or allowed to commit suicide. I met several prisoners like that myself. I can't imagine people of a different nationality having a similar attitude—they might not *want* to be captured, but if they were, they wouldn't demand death. But these men had been told that according to Japanese tradition there was no greater shame than being taken prisoner, and they believed it. They really did feel like they'd committed some kind of sin. Many of them felt they'd disgraced themselves to the point where they could never return to Japan, and that their life was already over. I'd say more than half of them felt that way.

Of course, this was all before the battle of Okinawa. Things were different after that. For the first time the Allies captured prisoners by the thousands, and for the first time people started to give up hope for Japan. I won't say people were happy to be taken prisoner, but those who were didn't seem to think it was their own fault.

Shiba   During Hideyoshi's invasion of Korea (1592–1598), there was a warrior who surrendered to the Korean side. In the Korean literature he's referred to as "Sayaka," but I believe that's a transliteration error for the Japanese name "Saemon." Anyway, in Korea it's said that he claimed to have surrendered because he'd long been attracted to Confucianism, but it's hard to imagine a Japanese warrior of that era feeling that way—things weren't quite so refined back then. My theory is

---

9. A quote from the WWII Imperial Japanese Military Code.

that he was a warrior from Tsushima[10] who didn't particularly want to fight against the Koreans, so he surrendered to their army as soon as he came up on shore. You'd expect a surrendering warrior to spend the rest of the war in a prison camp somewhere, but this guy soon became a general in the Korean army and actually led troops against the Japanese. What's interesting is that if you read the Japanese records of this event, they don't treat it as particularly remarkable. They certainly don't describe it as some kind of immoral act, which I think reflects how such behavior was seen during the Warring States period.

So at least up until the Meiji era it was conceivable that if you were taken prisoner you might even end up working for the enemy, and doing so wouldn't be strange at all. I suppose the Meiji government didn't want that to happen in wars with foreign enemies, though, so during the Russo–Japanese War they started telling soldiers to do their best not to be captured. And "do your best" is the key phrase here. People like Nogi Maresuke (1849–1912)[11] had a very broad-minded view of prisoners, on their side and the enemy side alike. The attitude was that you should avoid being taken prisoner, but sometimes circumstances would deliver you into the enemy's hands, and that was just the way things went. If you managed to escape and make it back, well good for you. That was Nogi's take on things. One example is Akiyama Yoshifuru (1859–1930), who established the Japanese cavalry that defeated the Cossacks. He was also the older brother of Akiyama Saneyuki, Masaoka Shiki's friend who we were talking about earlier. Anyway, one of the men under his command was taken prisoner, but escaped by jumping off a train on the Trans-Siberian Railway as it was crossing a bridge or something. When he made it back, Akiyama scolded him and said he wouldn't have been captured if he hadn't been so careless, but Nogi praised him.

---

10. An archipelago between the Korean peninsula and the Japanese island of Kyushu.

11. A general in the Imperial Japanese Army and governor of Taiwan.

In any case, in the Meiji era soldiers were farmers' kids and people like that, so if you didn't tell them to avoid being taken prisoner they'd do like they'd heard in stories and turn on you, like a captured piece in a game of shogi. I think that's where it all started.

Keene   I've read a bit about the Russo–Japanese War myself, and apparently even high-ranking Japanese officers were taken prisoner during that war. They made some interesting complaints to the International Red Cross at the time. One said something like, "Global treaties state that captured officers should be given the same food as soldiers in the opposing army, but what they're serving us is of poor quality." Another complained about not being permitted to go ice-skating on frozen lakes during the winter like the Russians were doing. "We all want to go skating—please do something," he wrote. The surviving letters from that time are all so charming.

Shiba   Right. Unlike the Japanese army that developed later, the army during the Russo–Japanese war followed international customs and law. Becoming a prisoner back then was just part of the game, a rule that you followed. It wasn't something you were ashamed of.

I was in a tank division during World War II, and I was taught to never leave my tank, even if it was burning. Our field manual said, "Your tank's fate is your fate." If our tank caught fire because a bullet hit a fuel line or something, the tank was to be our coffin. What a grim thought. The field manual for artillery units said something similar: "Your gun's fate is your fate; never leave its side." I guess the aim was to prevent soldiers from abandoning their artillery pieces and running away, but this all developed after the Russo–Japanese War. I imagine situations like that arose during that earlier war, so the higher-ups learned their lesson and made such behavior taboo, made it a moral issue. I remember I once spoke with an American who had been in a tank brigade during the war—he was a movie executive by the time we talked—and I don't know if this is true or not, but he said there was a sign inside his tank that said something like, "This tank has enough armor to stop such-and-such a shell, so don't worry—you're safe." I was so jealous! Our tanks might as well have been made out of tin. They hadn't been updated since 1938, after all. Not at all something I wanted to hang my own fate on.

I think all those people who blathered on about the "indomitable Japanese spirit," not to mention those who actually believed it, were a product of the early Showa era (1926–1989). That's when people started writing that sort of rhetoric, and when militaristic teachings started to pervade society. Nothing like that happened in the preceding Taisho era (1912–1926). Even during the Russo–Japanese War people seem to have been a bit more broad-minded.

Keene   There's a short story by Izumi Kyoka called *Kaijo Hatsuden* (A Telegram from Haicheng) that was published a little earlier, around the First Sino–Japanese War (1894–1895). In the story, a Japanese Red Cross worker who was taken prisoner tries to justify his situation. He says that he doesn't mind having been captured, that there's nothing bad about it. The story was published openly and didn't cause any problems at the time, but when Izumi Kyoka's collected works were republished around 1940, it wasn't included.

Shiba   Is that so? Well I guess that supports my point that the Japan of the Meiji period, around the time of the Russo–Japanese War, had a more enlightened, Westernized spirit. There was a greater sense that Japan was similar to the West. Then during the early Showa period, in a very short span up to 1945, that very dark, distinctly Japanese brand of nationalism arose. It's curious that leaders managed to present it as tradition, since Japanese history doesn't really support it.

Keene   Even more ironic is that it only took about ten years to fabricate

72   Chapter 4

an old tradition. Only ten years to convince the populace that this was all tradition stretching back to the days of Yamato[12].

Shiba   A mere decade.

Keene   Put another way, if you work at it for around a decade, you can invent a tradition.

Shiba   That's the scary thing about politics. The nationalism that was being praised in the World War II era was very German, with almost no relation to the traditions of Yamato.

The *Wako* Pirates

Shiba   As you know, from the mid-Muromachi era to the start of the Warring States period, pirates called *wako* ran rampant. Each group of pirates had its own specialty. The ones from Tsushima would attack Korea. Those from the Goto islands[13] headed for South China. But these pirates didn't have a good understanding of geography or economics. They didn't know where their loot would be desired, or where they could sell it for good prices—they didn't have trade information, in other words—so they needed someone higher up to direct them to the ports that would be most profitable. Well, the Chinese themselves sure could! One of the most famous was Wang Zhi, a castaway from Southern China. He became the captain of a band of wako who would sail around and do the fighting. It's like the pirates were his labor force and he was management, telling them where to go. And they made money doing so. So much money, in fact, that word got around that the Goto islands were full of riches, and people from all over Kyushu began heading there. The language that they spoke to communicate with each other became the Kyushu dialect. So by the end of the

---

12. An early name for Japan.
13. Part of modern-day Nagasaki prefecture.

Muromachi period, the common language of the Goto islands was the standardized language for all of Kyushu.

But getting back to the wako, for several months they controlled the Zhoushan islands in Hangzhou Bay. They fought a long, pitched battle with the Imperial Ming Army for the islands, which they won, and took the place over. You'd think that after all that they would make the islands their home, but they picked up and left after a few months. They moved on to some other city on the Chinese coast, which they again took over. I forget exactly where I read it, but some Chinese person from the time wrote, "Just leave them alone—they'll move along eventually." I'm not sure why they did that. Maybe they got homesick or something, or maybe the Japanese of the time didn't have much desire to actually "take over" places. So they never really learned how to do it, didn't develop the skills for governing occupied lands.

Also, even though rice was grown in southern China, huge famines occurred from time to time. In Japan there were monsoons—well, I guess southern China is in a monsoon region too—but back in Japan you'd have a good rainy season with just the occasional typhoon, and it was more livable and easier to grow rice there. Maybe the pirates left so they could eat rice again. [Laughs] But seriously, that would have been enough. It didn't take much to move them along. Anyway, this wako style of waging war strikes me as highly representative of the Japanese. Just rushing in, having a fight, and calling it done. Maybe you win, maybe you lose, but whatever. Just lick your wounds and move on.

Getting back to World War II—and I bring this up because you and I are old war comrades [Laughs]— the aerial attack on Pearl Harbor was led by a man from Nara prefecture named Fuchida Mitsuo (1902–1976)[14]. If you follow my family tree on my mother's side back

---

14. An air group commander under fleet commander Vice Admiral Nagumo Chuichi at the time, Fuchida was the aerial attack coordinator and flew a Type 97 (Nakajima B5N) torpedo bomber to lead the first wave of planes in the attack on Pearl Harbor.

far enough, I think we might be distantly related. Anyway, I recently had the opportunity to go out drinking with him, and he was quite an interesting fellow. Now I'm no militarist of course, and neither is he—actually, I think he's become a Christian minister or something like that—and from the beginning he'd argued that there was no way Japan could defeat the United States in a war. Sure, they could sink some boats, and he led three hundred planes to do just that, but before you go sinking boats you've got to consider what you're going to do *after* that, right? Surprisingly enough the Imperial Navy apparently hadn't thought that far ahead. Neither had the Japanese government, for that matter. They may have had some vague notions, like taking the southern Dutch Indies or grabbing some oil-producing land, but that was just a wish list, not a military strategy. They confused wanting oil fields with strategy, and didn't think through what would happen after they attacked Pearl Harbor.

Now Fuchida is a soldier to the bone, but he's also from the Kansai region, and we Kansai folk don't attach ourselves to ideals so readily. We're known as shrewd traders, and like in any business deal we're always asking what happens after the transaction. He told me he once let slip to an Imperial Navy elite something like, "Well, it doesn't matter since we're going to lose anyway, so let's just fight like the wako." He said this because the intent was just to attack Pearl Harbor, then maybe run some air raids on the U.S. coast and head home. That's it. That's how the wako waged war, after all. Japanese wars across Asia and the Pacific were all like that. Just bumbling into war with no clear purpose. It's all wako warfare.

The Russo–Japanese War is the one exception. That was another case of fighting an undefeatable foe, but at least the battlefield—Manchuria—was well defined geographically, and Japan could calculate how many troops Russia could mobilize via the Trans-Siberian Railroad. So at least they could get an idea of how things would turn out if they applied a bit of strategy, which for once they did. Betrayals might have taken place during the battle of Sekigahara and the Genpei War, like we talked about before, but that kind of thing wouldn't happen with Russia, so the Japanese could at least try to formulate some kind of specific strategy. But this really only happened in the Russo–Japanese War. The Pacific War was just a large-scale wako war.

Keene   Well I was in the U.S. Navy back then, and that's definitely not how we saw it. When I entered the Navy my commanding officer, a lieutenant commander, told us that we'd probably die in our uniforms. Not because we'd die in battle, but because everyone thought the war would go on for decades. Everyone was quite gloomy at the time.

Shiba   That is a depressing thought indeed.

CHAPTER 5

Confucianism and Japanese Morals

Japanese Rationalism

Shiba   I sometimes wonder where Japanese rationalism comes from. Is it inherent to the Japanese, or is it the result of contact with the West? I've thought about this for a long time. The issue is no doubt complex, but one example of what I'm talking about is Yamawaki Toyo (1705–1762), an Eastern medicine practitioner who lived in the mid-Edo period. He wasn't a scholar of the West—he was the court doctor at the palace in Kyoto, so of course he practiced Eastern medicine—but at the age of forty-nine he performed his first human dissection, at Awataguchi, in Kyoto. He'd wanted to perform a dissection for a long time, so he'd been practicing on otters and such, but he wasn't satisfied with that. As to why he so badly wanted to perform a dissection, as you know, Eastern medicine takes Wu Xing[1] as an absolute principle for all things, right? But only one human dissection had ever been conducted, back during the Song dynasty (960–1279). That happened because a Song government official gave permission for some famous doctor to perform the dissection and create an anatomy chart from it, and that anatomy chart made its way to Japan. When the doctor performed the dissection, however, he found that things weren't arranged in the way

---

1. The "five elements" used to describe many phenomena in Chinese philosophy.

78   Chapter 5

he'd been taught. In other words, they didn't follow the principles of
Wu Xing. But since that would have been an outrageous finding, and
since the subject of the dissection was a criminal, the doctor decided
the deviation must have been caused by the criminality of the speci-
men, and went ahead and created anatomy charts that were true to Wu
Xing. The result was a medical text that was based on ideals, not reality. Those erroneous anatomy charts crossed over to Japan, and ended
up in the hands of most of the Eastern medicine practitioners here.

Now Yamawaki had serious doubts about these Eastern texts, doubts
that he was trying to resolve with his otter dissections, but of course
otters are a little different from humans. After years of waiting, at the
age of forty-nine, he finally got permission to perform a human dissection. He was thrilled to confirm that the anatomy charts from China
were incorrect, and wrote up his findings in the *Zoshi* (On Internal
Organs), the first Japanese anatomy text. A number of rationalists
were coming onto the scene around the same time, although their lives
didn't precisely overlap with Yamawaki's. The Confucian philosopher
Ogyu Sorai (1666–1728) was one, and Motoori Norinaga (1730–1801)
was another. Well, Motoori may not have been a rationalist exactly,
but he was one of the first people to study something resembling
modern-day academic subjects, rather than ethics. The same goes for
Ogyu. Yamawaki was strictly an Eastern medicine practitioner, but he
was still part of the changes that were taking place at the time, in that
he started doubting the tenets of Wu Xing's ideal-based medicine and
took a step toward rationalism through his dissections.

I've always found it curious that the Japanese are like that. Even
today, I still wonder whether this rationalism arose from contact with
the Portuguese and the Spanish, or maybe the Dutch—there wasn't
much contact with these cultures, but maybe it was enough for rationalism to seep in—or whether, in contrast to the Chinese, the Japanese
have simply never clung to ideals. Most likely it's some combination

of both. Even when Japan was governed under the Chinese Ritsuryo code[2], a completely Chinese system was never adopted. The system of government was more pragmatic, never an all-in Confucian system in the truest sense. If you're going to follow Confucianism to the letter, then there are strictures about everything from how to interact with farmers to the strict ranking of family members, but those rigorous details of Confucianism never took root in Japan. All that was stuff for bookish folk who read the works of Confucius and Mencius (372?–289?); it never became part of lifestyle norms and customs, like wedding and funeral ceremonies and things like that. So Japan never went totally Confucian, and that was probably a big plus when making contact with Westerners.

Of course, you could also argue that China was the more rational country. You could certainly claim that Cheng-Zhu's school of thought[3] was analytical in a sense. Yet the more European stance of saying, "If it looks like a duck and quacks like a duck, then it probably is a duck" only entered one Asian country without resistance, and that was Japan.

Keene   That's very true. There are various theories as to why modern thought didn't develop in a similar way in China, but the most common explanation is Sinocentrism. In other words, the Chinese considered China to be the center of the world and other nations to be no more than peripheral barbaric states, so actively adopting ideas from those countries was inconceivable. Even after contact with Europeans, there was no sense among the Chinese that these people might have knowledge worth absorbing, that something could be learned from them.

---

2. Approximately the middle of the seventh century through the tenth century.
3. One of the major schools of neo-Confucianism, which did not admit for any external world apart from the material.

The Japanese, however, always had China as this highly developed neighbor, so they were accustomed to learning from other countries. That's probably why there was no particular resistance to the Portuguese when they first arrived. The Japanese looked at the things the Portuguese had and were able to recognize that they were superior to what they themselves had, without ever considering them unacceptable due to their foreignness. This was particularly true because Japan had just come out of the Warring States period. Social order had been completely disrupted and what was considered common sense shown to be untenable, so novel ideas were welcomed. People saw that guns were highly effective at killing enemies, so they quickly incorporated them in to military tactics. I think things would have been very different if this first contact had come just a little later—say around the middle of the Tokugawa era. As proof of that—well, I'm not sure whether this is actual proof—but as everyone knows, the Japanese developed a matchlock gun called the *tanegashima* from a similar Portuguese design. Oda Nobunaga used them and several gunsmiths made them for a while, but the technology was later abandoned. The Tokugawa shogunate didn't have gun battalions, for example, and didn't seem particularly interested in guns or cannons.

In other words, the attitude of acceptance towards all things foreign seems to have faded once a more fixed society evolved. Some individual Japanese were exceptions, namely those interested in Dutch studies, but the government, at least, appears to have taken much less interest in things from overseas. So it seems the Portuguese arrived at just the right time, as the Warring States period was ending. That was quite a lucky thing for Japan, since during that period the use of foreign things wasn't seen as corrupting.

Shiba   It didn't lead to exclusionism, or deification of the state.

Keene   Right. If society had been a bit more settled, like it did become later on, the Japanese most likely would have seen the use of foreign things as undignified or unbecoming.

The Japanese and Confucianism

Shiba   I'm exaggerating quite a bit here, but it seems to me that most ethnic groups in the world have acquired the wisdom that society can only develop if the populace is tamed using some absolute principle, be it Islam or Christianity or Confucianism or what have you. Otherwise, the society they belong to never would have developed. In China, for example, Confucianism held sway for some two thousand years, but when it became obvious that it didn't mesh with the modern age, Mao Zedong appeared. He didn't fanatically discipline people to follow new principles just to change the government; he used the state as a tool to train people regarding every aspect of their lives. Re-education, in other words. The period of Maoist education was brief, and for that reason it stands out quite clearly in hindsight, but normally this process happens over a long span of history. So for example an Islamic society eventually develops out of Islam, and that society becomes an Islamic state. Other countries and societies follow a similar developmental path as everyone just lives their lives pursuing their own happiness. But for some reason that doesn't seem to be the case for the Japanese. When we had a Confucian state, governmental systems were imported in form only, not content. Japanese emperors married relatives, for example. That was the case both before and after the Nara period (710–794). People in a truly Confucian state would have been quite shocked by that. They wouldn't even marry someone with the same family name, related or not. When I think about the fact that in Japan even the person at the apex of society—the emperor—was doing it, I wonder if we can really call what was practiced in Japan Confucianism. It makes me wonder if Confucian principles were ever

82   Chapter 5

really inculcated in the Japanese. In the Tokugawa era people did a fair amount of studying, but that's as far as it went. It didn't lead to changes in how we conduct funerals or things like that.

Keene   Well, in terms of how broadly or deeply Confucianism spread in Japan, I think it spread quite far during the Tokugawa period, and still has deep roots today. If a Japanese moral code does exist, it's certainly Confucian, not Buddhist. A friend recently told me that each year crime rates tend to go up in the cities of all advanced countries, with Japan as the sole exception. I think an old-fashioned Japanese person would be troubled by that; they'd wonder why crime doesn't go up in Japan as well. They'd masochistically want to catch up with other modern countries. [Laughs] Maybe in the end there's no specific reason for it, but if there were, I suspect it would be related to Confucianism. What do you think?

Shiba   I'm not sure how much I can agree with that. Buddhism isn't a form of morality, after all. Morality is a nearly meaningless concept in Buddhism. There's *vinaya*, the doctrines and strictures, but those aren't really morals in the ordinary sense of the word. Just learning the Five Constants[4] of Confucianism isn't enough to build a moral code. Morals are the ideals *behind* the strictures on how you hold your chopsticks and how you bow to others. Confucianism is all about daily order, but no amount of reading the Confucian classics is going to give you a moral code.

   In the case of the Chinese, even people who can hardly read or write are Confucian. I've long been impressed by how Confucian even Chinese rickshaw pullers and manual laborers are, far more so than any Japanese Confucian. I feel it's because of their powerful respect for integrity. They never betray others. I'm no expert on this, but I believe

---

4. The Confucian principle of *wuchang*, which stresses the importance of humaneness, justice, proper rites, knowledge, and integrity.

the Confucian concept of integrity emerged long after that of *li*, rites and rituals. Still, I think this moral code probably developed in China in response to a societal need particular to that nation. People could only rely on the government to a limited extent, and over thousands of years of unhelpful government they learned to rely on horizontal relationships like those between comrades, relatives, friends, and neighbors. When the need is absolute, and only integrity can meet it, that's when you've attained true Confucianism.

Yet under the *han* system[5] in Japan, Confucian scholars were assigned to each domain—one or two for smaller domains, three or four for larger ones—and that was pretty much the extent of Confucianism. Sure, manners had Confucian aspects to them, like the truly bizarre ones established in the Muromachi period by the Ogasawara clan, an extension of the Ashikaga shogunate. For instance, when a couple got married, gifts had to be given to the bride's family, and the person delivering the gifts had to say specific things. Or when eating, your chopsticks had to be used in a certain way. The shoguns of that time came up with all of these meaningless rituals purely as a way to keep a bunch of savage daimyo in check. There were no principles behind them—it was all just banality used as a tool to force restraint. It had nothing to do with Confucian principles.

During the Tokugawa period people finally had enough time to sit down and read books, and they actually did start to read. People like Rai San'yo (1780–1832), who was a Confucian himself but realized that the way he and his contemporaries interacted with relatives and friends didn't follow Confucian principles at all. Maybe it's odd to give just Rai San'yo as an example, but I do feel like Confucianism had almost no influence on people here.

---

5. A system of warrior estates in feudal Japan lasting from the Edo period until the early Meiji period. Han domains were the precursors of modern-day prefectures.

84   Chapter 5

The Role of Shame

Shiba   So given that, how has social order been maintained so well? I think it's because people are afraid of embarrassing themselves. They don't want to say anything that would cause them to be laughed at or bring shame upon themselves. As the kids say these days, it's about being "cool" or "uncool." The warriors of Kamakura had already defined cool—showing enemies your back on the battlefield was uncool, so never retreat. But that's aesthetics, not morality. Maybe aesthetics isn't quite the right word to use, but I'll use it for lack of a better one. I wonder if there's any country other than Japan where society held together for so long purely on the basis of aesthetics. I guess we're still a developing country in terms of our crime rate [Laughs], but that's because criminal activity is considered uncool here.

The reason people don't commit crimes is because doing so would bring shame on their parents or embarrass them among their friends. That's enough to hold back most people here. It seems unrelated to a fear of God or a consideration of the natural state of human relationships as set forth in Confucianism.

Keene   Of course no ideals related to a God or gods exist in Confucianism, and they didn't exist in the Japan of long ago either. But to give a silly example, say a burglar robs a store, kills an elderly woman in the process, and is later caught. He's interrogated and eventually confesses to the crime. In Japan, a person in that situation will always say, "I'm sorry," or "I've done a terrible thing," right? That's what I always read in the papers, at least. Is that just what newspapers like to print? I think in other countries criminals deny they've committed a crime. They rarely confess. And if they do, it's reluctantly and without apologies. In Japan—at least according to the newspapers—even the perpetrator of the most horrible murder or robbery or kidnapping will admit to their crimes and apologize in very Confucian terms. It's not that they feel they've sinned against any god, but because they feel guilt towards society.

Shiba   Maybe not so much society as the public.

Keene   The public, yes. And Confucianism is the philosophy of the public. It's not that the Japanese avidly study the writings of Confucius and Mencius and have become Confucians as a result, but I do believe they've subtly absorbed those ideals, perhaps through watching kabuki theater and things like that. Or they would, for example, see the puppet theater of Chikamatsu Monzaemon (1653–1725) and unconsciously adopt its attitudes toward double suicide as their own.

Shiba   Okay, I get what you're saying. A sort of public standard exists that determines what they feel shame in comparison to, and it's a Confucian standard. Got it.

Keene   Japanese people often speak of the balance between obligation and human emotion, but those terms don't come from Buddhism or Shinto. I don't think they come from aesthetics, either. If anything, they're Confucian, right? And if you consider the tragedies of Chikamatsu to be about obligation and human emotion, it seems that his spectators somehow accepted those moralistic ideals as their own.

Shiba   But there are counterexamples, too. When Francis Xavier arrived at Bonotsu in Satsuma[6], the boat he arrived on was scheduled to leave port a week later, so he sent a report of his first week of observations in a letter to the Spanish king. In that report he clearly took the Satsuma people as representative of all Japanese, which I suppose was a good enough choice, since they were indeed very Japanese. But still, these were uneducated folk, not too far removed from the Hayato people we discussed before. Anyway, in his report Xavier wrote that the

6. Modern-day Kagoshima prefecture.

86   Chapter 5

people of Satsuma often used the word *hazukashii* [ashamed], and that they were highly self-controlled.

Later, actually much later, in the early Tokugawa period, a Chinese scholar at Edo Castle received an envoy from the Joseon (Korean) government who'd come on a mission to Japan. They communicated by writing in Chinese, though the Korean envoy was much more skilled. The Japanese scholar had quite poor Chinese, in fact. Anyway, the envoy wrote, "I hear that you have no need for police in your country." When the scholar asked what he meant, the envoy added, "Because your criminals kill themselves before the police can arrive." The scholar—I suppose it was one of the Hayashi clan who served as Daigaku no kami[7] or someone like that—fumbled about for an answer, and finally came up with, "No, that's only the custom in Satsuma. They consider being arrested shameful, so they condemn themselves. For that reason there's no need to send police." The whole thing was based on shame, on not being able to face society. Criminals there didn't necessarily think what they'd done was wrong, but they knew the public would reject their actions, so they committed seppuku. But that only happened in Satsuma, the scholar told the envoy.

Even so, I'd like to think that the people of Satsuma served as something of a model for later Japanese. The air of old Kamakura hung about the place, more so than elsewhere. And if that's the case, then they weren't reading the Confucian classics. Doing so would have been discouraged; during the Edo period, even warriors in Satsuma were taught to avoid reading because it made them think too much. You may be right that Confucianism crept in through kabuki and bunraku puppetry and spread from there, but the people Xavier encountered in Satsuma lived before all that happened, and even during the early Tokugawa period they would have been the farthest removed from any

---

7. The court position of head of the Imperial University. The position was hereditary within the Hayashi clan from the seventeenth century until its abolishment in the Meiji era.

Confucian influence. But still, that's the way the people of Satsuma, or in other words the Japanese, behaved.

Keene   But I don't think you can say Satsuma was removed from Confucianism. When Fujiwara Seika (1561–1619)[8] decided to study Confucianism, Satsuma was the first place he went.

Shiba   He did, didn't he. Wow, you know all about this. This is why I need to be careful when I'm talking to you. [Laughs] But I think he went to Bonotsu because he wanted to get to China. He didn't particularly want to be in Satsuma, but Chinese ships followed a route between Hangzhou and Bonotsu, via Ryukyu[9] or wherever. Yeah, I believe it was Ryukyu. Anyway, I think Fujiwara was just looking for a ship to take.

Keene   Well, not to press the point, but when Fujiwara arrived in Bonotsu and realized that he couldn't make it to China, he didn't express any regret. He discovered that the books he wanted to study existed in Japan, and went back to Kyoto a happy man.

Shiba   Yes, he did. He discovered them in Bonotsu. And I guess that implies many books about Confucianism had arrived there. [Laughs]

Incidentally, Fujiwara was invited to visit daimyo all over the country, but he was a difficult man and would only visit those he liked. He also never took a daimyo as a patron, and remained independent his entire life. Maeda Toshiie (1538–1599), one of the first lords of Kaga province, often invited him for lectures. I'm not sure exactly what they talked about, but I suspect in modern terms it resembled maxims for living. Maeda wasn't an educated man, so highly intellectual talks wouldn't have been much use to him. I assume Fujiwara's teachings were along the lines of, "If you act this way, this will be the result." But that was enough to impress a man of the Warring States period,

---

8. A neo-Confucian scholar of the Edo period.
9. Modern-day Okinawa.

88   Chapter 5

so much so that Maeda told a favorite underling of his, Kato Kiyomasa (1561–1611), "You've got to invite this guy Fujiwara over and listen to what he has to say—I've never heard such wisdom." Of course "wisdom" in this case was more like life skills than lofty learning. I believe Fujiwara presented his teachings in the form of common-sense morals. That was enough to deeply impress someone like Maeda, which is why I don't think Confucianism had really spread all that much. What do you think?

Keene   The situation was probably something like that. But I still think Confucianism had a strong influence at the time, and that its influence remains strong today. Even if you look at juvenile delinquents in Japan these days, they seem to have a very different attitude toward their parents than American delinquents do.

Shiba   You're even impressed by our juvenile delinquents?

Keene   I am. [Laughs]

Reliance on Others

Shiba   Actually, I have one vexing problem with the state of Japanese morality. Confucianism taught us one set of morals, but I want to know if any home-grown moral code developed here in Japan.

For example, take Shinran's theory of *akunin shoki*[10]. He wrote, "if the good can be reborn in paradise, how much more so the wicked." An American army information officer who was visiting Kyoto in 1945 heard this and found it to be a very unappealing idea, because it seemed to promote evil over good, and as long as people believed it they couldn't be saved. He called up a bunch of people to explain it to him, but I guess none of them gave him a satisfactory response, because for

---

10. A tenet in Jodo Shinshu Buddhism that states evil people are the Buddha's primary targets for salvation.

whatever reason my turn came around. Don't get me wrong—he was quite gentlemanly about it. His attitude was, "I'd really like to understand this, can you please come help me?" So I went, wondering why he'd summon a cub reporter like me instead of a monk or whatever. Anyway, I found myself doing the best I could, trying to explain Shinran's theory of akunin shoki through an interpreter. The American's concept of morality was of course one he got from Christianity, so the conversation couldn't get beyond how this concept negated his own sense of morality. I, on the other hand, thought of "evil" as similar to original sin, something you can't just get rid of. For example, you might not expect an extremely lustful, materialistic person to be capable of entering paradise, but the Amitabha Buddha of Jodo Shinshu Buddhism will save even such a person. That's the joyous sentiment expressed in the Jodo Shinshu chant *namu amida butsu*. I did my best to explain all that, but it didn't really get to the question of morality as he'd hoped it would. In the end I told him he'd have to ask someone else, and left.

I've been thinking about it ever since ... although not deeply. It's as though Japan has become placid to the point that there's no need to think deeply. We're just a bunch of people living in this odd island nation, crowded in by our neighbors, our worries not extending beyond what we're having for dinner. So we have this society that's stabilized itself just by virtue of people being afraid to embarrass themselves. It's a strange nation, insofar as that's all it takes to maintain society. For me, that's always been the strangest aspect of Japan.

Keene   The Japanese often explain aspects of their culture by referring to the small size of the country, but maybe that's just because long ago they were comparing themselves to their neighbor China, and later to America. Those countries are indeed much larger than Japan, but consider the Netherlands. I believe it has less than one-tenth the land area

90   Chapter 5

of Japan, and an even higher population density. So perhaps we should ask why the Japanese and Dutch cultures are so very different, despite both being small, crowded nations.

Also, getting back to the idea of akunin shoki, I find Shinran's explanation of it quite clear. I've never felt any resistance to it, at least. In fact, I found it to be a wonderful description from the first time I read it. In my view, those who call themselves "good" are suspect. I've always thought that people convinced of their own goodness will have the hardest time making it to paradise [Laughs], and I imagine Shinran assumed the same. A person like that will build a temple or a splendid pagoda somewhere and be convinced they've secured their place in paradise, without ever making a real effort. But they're the least likely to make it. Evil people, on the other hand, have spent their life performing ill deeds, and know from the start that they won't make it to paradise without help. But through reliance on the strength of the Amitabha Buddha, it becomes possible. I find that idea very easy to understand. But I can see how a Western Protestant with profound faith would have a hard time grasping the concept. Protestantism is a self-help religion, and the Dutch in particular had strong ideas about the importance of self-help. The dedicated efforts of Dutch merchants turned a nearly worthless province with no resources into a powerful nation. For societies like that, an ideal that advocates relying on the strength of others is hard to comprehend.

Western Art and Eastern Morality

Shiba   Speaking of the Netherlands, in your book *The Japanese Discovery of Europe* you discuss Honda Toshiaki (1744–1821)[11], who considered the Netherlands to be the greatest nation in the world.

---

11. An expert on mathematics, astronomy, and navigation who also wrote about economics and the colonization of Ezo (modern-day Hokkaido and nearby islands).

And at the end of the Tokugawa shogunate, Sakamoto Ryoma (1836–1867)[12] went to some academy in the backwoods of Kochi to hear a lecture about the Dutch Constitution. It makes me laugh to imagine what kind of translation the professors at that school came up with, but later Sakamoto also heard a lecture about the American constitution, and was so impressed he became a revolutionary. Anyway, I get the impression that the Netherlands was quite hard for the Japanese to comprehend. Ando Shoeki (1703?–1762)[13] apparently considered the Netherlands to be an ideal nation too, so I suppose Honda wasn't the only one who thought of it as a nation of saints. That's what he called it, right?

Keene   Right, he couldn't understand how the Dutch could be so wonderful if they were ordinary humans like the rest of us.

Shiba   Yeah, his writings get very strange. He said we Japanese are clearly fools since we live in houses made of grass and wood, while truly clever humans live in homes of stone and metal. I'm not sure where he came up with that, but his idea was that if the Japanese could reach the point of conducting long-distance overseas trade like the Dutch, then they too could all live in stone houses. It's amusing that most Japanese these days do indeed live in stone houses. [Laughs]

This was long after Honda's days, but when Katsu Kaishu (1823–1899)[14] returned from America full of new knowledge, he became close friends with an idealist from Kumamoto named Yokoi Shonan (1809–1869). Yokoi had some very dangerous ideas for the time, and since the only foreign language he could read was Chinese—he knew no Dutch, of course—he went to Katsu to learn what was going on in the world.

---

12. One of the instigators behind the overthrow of the Tokugawa shogunate.

13. An eccentric eighteenth-century philosopher.

14. A statesman, naval engineer, and captain of the first Japanese vessel to sail to the Western world (San Francisco).

92   Chapter 5

There he heard about the presidential system in the United States. Yokoi said, "That sounds like the perfect state," and Katsu praised him for it. Katsu said he was a fast learner, someone who could quickly penetrate to the heart of a situation. So from the mid-Edo period the image Japanese intellectuals had of the West—not everyone, mind you, but the ones who really understood things—was that China wasn't the only place with saints. Some allowed that idea to overcome their past bias and become Christians. It had been drilled into everyone's head that Christianity was evil, so I imagine people like Yokoi and others were afraid to convert, but I feel he had to really work hard to restrain himself.

One example from the late Tokugawa shogunate is Kido Takayoshi (1833–1877) of the Choshu domain[15], a *shishi* anti-shogunate activist and later a statesman who was quite representative of the Meiji era. He visited Europe as soon as the Meiji Restoration took effect, and after an extensive tour almost like a sightseeing trip, he returned to Japan via the United States. Fukuchi Gen'ichiro (1841–1906)[16] and others well versed in matters concerning the West were on the same boat with him, so I believe Kido gained some understanding of what he was seeing, and during the trip he became enamored with the republican form of government. This is interesting because despite formally having been a vigorous supporter of the imperial system, he later decided that Japan's future was as a republic, that this new form of government would help Japan become a rich and powerful nation. Upon his return he seemingly changed his mind and went back to supporting imperial rule, in part, I think, because of the Christian problem. During an incident in Nagasaki, some Catholics were taken to a place called Otome Pass in Tsuwano[17], and killed. Kido was the man responsible for that. So you

---

15. Modern-day Yamaguchi prefecture.
16. Translator, journalist, playwright, and politician.
17. A town in modern-day Shimane prefecture.

have this revolutionary who later came to desire a republican government, but when it came to the Christians he just couldn't be true to himself. Even as he was going on about how wonderful the West and the Netherlands were, he may have been afraid that he might end up becoming a Christian himself if he wasn't careful.

Keene In Honda's writing, every time he mentions Christianity it's to make some disparaging remark about it. Yet he also writes that some 1,789 years earlier a very wise emperor of Rome spread a Wondrous Teaching—and here he writes "Wondrous Teaching" using the same term that Nichiren Buddhism uses to refer to the Lotus Sutra—that made the West into a great power, and he imagines how great it would be if Japan could also have such a Wondrous Teaching. The Wondrous Teaching he's referring to here can of course only be Christianity. [Laughs]

Shiba It's ironic that all these men who became government ministers after the Meiji Restoration supposedly hated Christianity, yet they adopted a civil code modeled after France's, which included monogamous marriage. I don't know if it was because they failed to realize such laws came from Christianity, or because they thought once Christianity was transformed into the technicality of law it was harmless, but it's interesting nonetheless that they could do that without much hesitation. This gets back to my long-held belief that the Japanese are insensitive to principles. If they had seriously considered what they were doing and realized that it was institutionalized Christianity, they might as well have made the government of the Meiji Restoration a Christian one. They could have made Christianity the national religion, but instead of taking the trunk itself they just grabbed a few of the branches. I suppose it was the convenient thing to do at the time, but if you look at it the other way around you could also say we're a people without principles.

94   Chapter 5

Keene   Another point to consider is that while the Japanese recognized that various wonderful things existed in China that didn't exist in Japan, they also believed Japan had its own wonderful things that couldn't be found in China. In particular, people considered *makoto* [sincerity] to be uniquely Japanese. Not that they had any proof that the Chinese lacked makoto—it seems they just wanted to believe Japan had something China didn't. Yamazaki Ansai (1619–1682)[18] shared this view. The scholar Sakuma Shozan (1811–1864) stressed the concept of "Eastern morals, Western technology." I guess it was clear that Western technology was ahead of Japan's, but I don't know what basis he had for concluding that Eastern morality was superior to that of the West. My suspicion is that he simply wanted to claim that there was something in the East—and by "East" he likely meant both China and Japan—that couldn't be found in the West.

Shiba   For self-respect. Where would we be without at least something?

Keene   In any case, just by looking at a machine you can tell, for example, that a Western steam locomotive is faster than traditional Japanese transport—a palanquin, in other words—but morality can't be measured as clearly, so it's possible to claim that Eastern morality is superior. I think the ultimate goal in Meiji Japan was to adopt ideas from the West while still retaining some ancient Asian or Japanese moral code. But I wonder just what that code was.

Shiba   I think Sakuma's claim was quite intentional. Ironically, I believe the most wonderful thing about the Japanese is the very same peculiarity I pointed out before—that we don't cling to burdensome principles. So, what's Japanese? Just these islands we live on. Japan is like a big plate, and it's interesting because there are so many dishes you can serve up on it. But that's a subject we could talk about endlessly, so

---

18. Founder of the Suika school of Shintoism.

let's discuss it again later when the opportunity presents itself. Before that, I'd like to change the topic, if you don't mind.

Keene   Go right ahead.

CHAPTER 6

Westerners in Japan

Tsuwano

Shiba   I hear that you took a trip to Tsuwano[1]. How was it? Tsuwano is of course the hometown of the novelist Mori Ogai (1862–1922), who if I recall correctly started learning Dutch from his father when he was still in kindergarten. I presume his father knew Dutch because he learned medicine in that language, but still it seems odd to me to begin foreign language studies at such a young age. Ogai was also nearly neighbors with Nishi Amane (1829–1897), so we have these two men who helped bring Japan into the modern age living just across the river from each other. It's interesting that the same era and province also produced Fukuba Bisei (1831–1907), a Japanese classics scholar in the Hirata school[2] who later headed the Department of Shinto Affairs or something like that. He was also part of the anti-Buddhist movement in the early Meiji era. So he was this highly pro-Japan, ultra-nationalist figure who went so far as to say Japan should expunge Buddhism. I definitely think that the anti-Buddhist movement was the Meiji government's biggest mistake. Thankfully it died out shortly after it began, but not before many precious buildings and statues were destroyed. Anyway, I think it's very interesting that a backwoods domain like

---

1. A town in modern-day Shimane prefecture famous as a site of Christian persecution in the Edo period.
2. Followers of the work of Hirata Atsutane (1776–1843), considered one of the great scholars of Japanese nativist studies.

98   Chapter 6

Tsuwano produced both a figure like this, and two men who were extremely knowledgeable about modern Europe and who advanced the modernization of Japan during the Meiji period.

Keene   I was quite surprised myself when I saw the exhibits at a local history museum there. I guess it wouldn't have been too surprising to find books written in Dutch, but they also had books in English, French, German, and Russian. Apparently one local got his Ph.D. at a German university, and his diploma, written entirely in Latin, was on display. The science room had a sign in French that said *"Chambre de Science,"* written in Nishi Amane's own hand. It was all quite international.

Shiba   I think the region started leaning in that direction around the middle of the Edo period[3]. Tsuwano was one of nearly three hundred domains, a small one that only produced around 50,000 *koku*[4], which meant that its residents couldn't really start up any kind of industry— they were too constrained by lack of resources. So around the mid-Edo period they looked to academics, and did everything they could to make the domain a center of scholarly learning. Many domains of that scale were much more enthusiastic about academia than the bigger ones—Uwajima in Iyo province[5], for example, and Obi in Hyuga province[6]. Obi was a very small domain headed by a daimyo named Ito, but it nevertheless produced many famous people. In southwestern Honshu there was Iwakuni[7], and of course Tsuwano. Uwajima was a minor domain during the late Tokugawa shogunate, but it was the place to be for Dutch studies[8]. Echizen Ono[9] was another center of

---

3. An alternate name for the period of the Tokugawa shogunate.
4. The *koku* is a traditional unit of measurement defined as enough rice to feed one person for one year (considered to be around 280 liters or 150 kilograms). Before the Meiji Restoration, feudal provinces were evaluated according to their potential for rice production in *koku*, with the largest holdings producing over one million *koku* of rice or its equivalent each year.
5. Modern-day Ehime prefecture.

Western learning run by a minor daimyo, though it's been largely forgotten today.

Keene Fukuchiyama[10] was like that too.

Shiba Right. Everyone was going to places like that to study, not just to Edo [Tokyo] and other big cities. Echizen Ono was particularly famous as a place to study what today we would call gymnastics, though it sounds funny to say that. Gymnastics was considered a part of medicine at the time, and no medical education was complete without learning something about it, so you'd go to Echizen Ono, where a famous lecturer taught. For various reasons Edo was the cultural center of Japan during the Edo period, but most of the academic learning was taking place out in rural areas. Osaka was definitely more of a center for Western learning than Edo.

Keene It seems like Kyoto wasn't, though.

Shiba Right, Kyoto had an aversion to Western learning—too many aristocratic families and Buddhist monks and the like. Kyoto had something like three thousand temples if you include the minor ones, and if you figure three monks per temple that's almost ten thousand right there. That doesn't make for a city overflowing with enthusiasm for Western academics.

Keene When I visited Tsuwano I was surprised by the academics there, but visiting the museums I was also surprised by the number of

---

6. Modern-day Miyazaki prefecture.
7. Modern-day Yamaguchi prefecture.
8. During this period "Dutch studies" (*Rangaku*) referred specifically to the study of the Dutch language and the technology and culture being brought to Japan from the Netherlands. The term's meaning later expanded to incorporate the study of all things Western.
9. In modern-day Fukui prefecture.
10. A city in northern Kyoto prefecture.

displays related to the martial arts. I think the common understanding is that martial arts practice started dying out in the late Tokugawa period, as the warriors themselves descended into decadence. But looking at the displays, I could see that martial arts studies were still going strong, even in the smaller domains.

Shiba   The people there probably considered martial training to be some kind of emotional support. By the way, you probably noticed that geographically speaking, Tsuwano looks something like a *noborigama* climbing kiln.

Keene   Right, right.

Shiba   It has this long valley floor, with a kind of large plateau to the south. That plateau was part of Choshu domain. So Choshu was sort of looking down on Tsuwano, and there was this feeling that they could just take the place in a day if they wanted to. Anytime some change came to Japan and got Choshu up in arms, Tsuwano would have to go along with them. The geography of the place prevented Tsuwano from having any desire whatsoever to fight Choshu, so those practicing martial arts must have had mixed feelings about it all, since there was no way they could win a defensive battle. They probably went on practicing with their bows and swords with no intent of actually using those skills. Like I said, the border was a plateau, and if the Choshu army came spilling down that hill Tsuwano wouldn't have had a chance. So I imagine the samurai of Tsuwano went ahead and practiced martial arts as was expected of them, but also took a keen interest in academics, since that was one way they could show up the bigger provinces. I wonder if that was one motivation for people like Nishi Amane and Mori Ogai.

Keene   Nishi Amane was one of the few late-Tokugawa scholars to actually study in the Netherlands, wasn't he? Others, like Fukuzawa

Yukichi (1835–1901), didn't seem to see much use in learning Dutch, and learned English instead. But Nishi stuck with Dutch to the end. He seems to have thought that anything important written in another language would eventually be translated into Dutch, so that was the best language to know.

Shiba   Murata Zoroku (1824–1869), the farmer who later became known as Omura Masujiro, said the same thing. Murata took classes in Dutch studies at the school established by Ogata Koan[11], where he was studying medicine, and he was proud of his knowledge of the West and his Dutch language ability throughout his life. Even so, he could only read and write Dutch —he couldn't speak it. But eventually English came to dominate, so when he was in Edo and he heard about James Curtis Hepburn (1815–1911)[12]—the same Hepburn who's famous for his system of romanizing Japanese words—he went to Dr. Hepburn to learn English. At the time Omura was still a retainer for the shogunate, but his background was very complex. He came from a family of farmers, which technically prevented him from becoming a Choshu domain clansman, but he did so well in his studies that the shogunate made him a samurai. Even so, either his English lessons with Dr. Hepburn didn't go very well, or maybe he'd studied Dutch so much when he was younger that he couldn't cram any English into his head, but whatever the reason, in the end he gave up. He said that pretty much everything one might want to know about medicine or anything else was written in Dutch or would be translated into it, so to know Dutch was to know the world.

---

11. Also known as Ogata Academy, Tekitekijuku Academy, and Tekijuku Academy.
12. An American doctor and Presbyterian missionary who first went to Japan in 1859 and contributed greatly to developing modern Western medical practice there.

The Ogata Koan Academy

Keene   Was the level of Dutch taught at the Ogata Academy high?

Shiba   Well, it's hard to measure according to modern standards, but it was likely taught the way Latin is, as a purely written language. It's not like they had many opportunities to actually speak it. Luckily, all it takes to understand Dutch is some grammatical knowledge—although I probably shouldn't say that in front of you, since I know you're skilled at Dutch yourself—so teachers just focused on grammar. The school also taught medicine, but focused almost exclusively on pathology. Everything else was left to the students to learn on their own, from experience. Pathology at least was described in Dutch books, so the more of those books the students read, the better they came to understand the language. When he later became the headmaster at the Ogata Academy, Omura Masujiro called himself ... well, he could have used a Japanese word for "lead instructor" or "principal" or something like that, but he called himself the "master." How would you pronounce that in Dutch?

Keene   Like "*may-ster.*"

Shiba   Right, well he pronounced this in a Japanese fashion and made it "*masutaa.*" So he calls himself *masutaa* and later on Fukuzawa Yukichi was called that as well. After Fukuzawa left the Ogata Academy he was the preeminent Dutch scholar in Japan, and boldly set off to make his mark in Edo, which allowed him to visit Yokohama for the first time. The treaty port[13] there was something like an international exposition for the Japanese of the time, where people would go to see all the curious sights. It was like a window on the world. The merchant houses hadn't all been built yet, and the streets were filled

---

13. "Treaty ports" were government-designated trade ports and areas of extraterritoriality for citizens of trade nations.

with stinking horse manure and turned to mud when it rained, but there were all these odd things from overseas on display, and foreigners walking about, so apparently a lot of people from Edo came to see the sights. Fukuzawa Yukichi visited right after he arrived.

But when he got there, he found that despite all his studies, he couldn't read any of the signs in front of the trade houses. He had been a Western studies student at the best school in Japan, so he'd felt sure he'd be able to read everything. He'd figured that mastering Dutch would allow him to understand all the languages of the world, including those of Europe and America and everywhere else, but these English signs were incomprehensible. Not that he even knew what language it was at first. That first visit was just a day trip, so I imagine he asked a local for help. In any case I'm sure he returned to Edo in shock over the fact that everything was in English rather than Dutch. So he simply switched to learning English. In that respect Fukuzawa was different from Nishi Amane and Omura Masujiro—he was still young and had an open mind. He saw that learning English would be the path to understanding the world, so he started studying it.

Keene   It almost makes you feel sorry for the Dutch at Dejima[14]. The Japanese had been studying Dutch for so long, thinking that the Netherlands was the center of the Western world, but now they were abandoning Dutch in favor of English. I'm sure that didn't make the Dutch happy.

Shiba   The Japanese didn't realize how small the Netherlands was until the signing of the Ansei Treaties[15], which established international relations between the two countries. Yes, I'm sure this was much

---

14. An artificial island in the bay of Nagasaki that served as the principal Dutch trading post from 1641–1853.

15. A series of treaties signed in 1858 opening Japan to trade with the Netherlands, the United States, Great Britain, Russia, and France.

104   Chapter 6

to the chagrin of the Dutch in Nagasaki.

By the way, a group of Japanese doctors visited the Netherlands in October 1969. Many of their grandfathers and great-grandfathers had studied Dutch medicine, and they were themselves professors at medical schools. The group leader was Dr. Ogata Tomio, the great-grandson of Ogata Koan. Among those accompanying him was Dr. Fujino Tsunesaburo, a famous microbiologist at Osaka University and the grandson of a man from Echizen who had studied cholera under Koan. Another was Dr. Otori Ranzaburo, a professor of medical history at Keio University and the grandson of Otori Keisuke, one of Koan's students. Ranzaburo was the younger brother of the wife of literary critic Kawakami Tetsutaro. He had studied Dutch medicine and became a professor after graduating from Keio University's medical school, and went on to study medical history, in particular the history of Dutch medicine. I had a chance to go drinking with this group in Akasaka or somewhere, and had a fine time. It was like reliving a scene from over a century ago. As everyone enjoyed their drinks I wondered who was going to pick up the tab, and it ended up being this man named Ito. He was the only one who wasn't a doctor, but he was the great-grandson, or maybe it was the great-great-grandson, of Ito Genboku, who was a Western practitioner and court doctor during the Tokugawa shogunate. Now the great-grandson is president of a cosmetics company called Papilio, a family business. I suppose there's some connection between Western medicine and cosmetics, but anyway they've been running this company since the Meiji period. Some of the other people who studied Dutch medicine established universities—Juntendo University for one, and Keio University. Those are the only two schools in Japan that offer degrees in medical history. No national universities do. I guess you could call them post-Dutch universities. So anyway, that night I drank on the Papilio Company's dime, or in a sense on Ito Genboku's. That really gave me a sense of the extent of the Dutch tradition in Japanese medicine.

So this was the group that went to the Netherlands in October 1969. Otori Ranzaburo had some physical limitations that made travel difficult, but he said he wanted to go because he was named after the place[16]. When they got there they attended a conference and a reception, and learned that the Dutch themselves had no idea how much they had contributed to Japan. In that sense, it's a big country, big enough to have forgotten how much it gave us. Those in the group who studied medical history were really looking forward to the trip, thinking they would learn a lot from scholars there about Dutch–Japanese relations, but they ended up being the ones doing the teaching. The Japanese feel that they owe an enormous debt to the Netherlands, but as far as the Dutch are concerned that debt seems to have been completely forgotten.

Keene   Well, to the Japanese the Netherlands seemed for a long time to be practically the only European country. But while the Dutch no doubt considered Dejima important, they had actual colonies on islands further to the west, like in Batavia[17] and throughout the Dutch East Indies, and that's where the real money was coming from. So except for scholars with some particular interest in the topic, I don't imagine much is done on Dutch–Japanese relations there. Besides medicine, the Japanese also learned oil painting, copperplate engraving, and many other things from the Dutch. Those aren't things that could only have been learned from them, but the Dutch just happened to be the ones to introduce them to Japan. Who knows, maybe the British would have done an even better job, but as luck had it, only the Dutch stuck around. The Portuguese and the Spanish were driven out, and even the Dutch wondered whether it was in the national interest

---

16. The *ran* in *Ranzaburo* is the same character used in *Oranda*, meaning the Netherlands.
17. Modern-day Jakarta, Indonesia.

106   Chapter 6

to maintain their trading post at Dejima. They probably made more money by smuggling goods.

Shiba   Yeah, it was probably hard to make much profit through official channels under the trade restrictions of that time. The only advantage was that gold didn't fetch the kind of price here that it did back in Europe. The Japanese didn't consider gold and silver as exactly equivalent, but there wasn't a huge difference between them. So the Dutch could bring silver in and cheaply trade it with the Japanese for gold. That was probably where most of the money came in through official channels.

Keene   The fact that Japanese copper contained a lot of gold was also important, since Japanese metalsmiths apparently still didn't know how to smelt it out. So the Dutch would buy large quantities of cheap copper and extract the gold from it. But the biggest moneymaker of all was probably smuggling. Anyway, the important point is that the Dutch in Nagasaki were traders, not academics. I've read excerpts from the journal of the Dutch trade house at Dejima, and it's filled with entries like, talking about being invited to the Suwa Shrine festival[18], "I've no intention of attending such a tedious affair. Besides, I'll be busy going over the books here that day." The traders there expressed no interest in Japanese culture, not even curiosity. They didn't even seem interested in finding out what kind of city Nagasaki was. They were just interested in all the money they would make in exchange for the inconvenience of their two-year stint there. There were only a few examples of actually intelligent Dutch who bothered thinking about Japanese–Dutch relations. One of them was Hendrik Doeff (1764–1837), the trade commissioner there for a time. He was the Dutch trader who spent the most time in Japan, and his take on trade

---

18. *Nagasaki Kunchi*, the largest festival in Nagasaki.

between Japan and the Netherlands was that Japan didn't really need to import anything, that the Japanese were already able to produce everything they needed to live happy lives. Furthermore, he believed the Dutch didn't really need anything from Japan. It's interesting that despite that, trade continued at Dejima for three hundred years.

Shiba   Doeff likely had his own reasons for staying at Dejima for so long. He's the one who created the Doeff–Halma dictionary, right? It's hard to overestimate how helpful that dictionary was in the modernization of Japan at the end of the Tokugawa shogunate. There were no printed editions—they were all copied by hand, and students of Dutch studies would make a copy to pay for their studies. I'm not sure how much they would get for doing that, but it was at least enough to buy a small house. So there's one good thing about being a student of Dutch studies—an excellent part-time student job!

The Doeff–Halma dictionary was a very precious thing. Maybe it's going too far to call the Ogata Koan Academy the Mecca of Western learning of the time, but it was certainly a major center of activity, and yet even that school had only one copy. The book had its own special room, separate from where the students were—you can still go and see it today—and it was never to be removed, it had to be used there. Students up studying all night would carry candles through the halls, going to the dictionary room to look up words and then returning to their own room. They called it the "Doeff Room," after the dictionary it contained, and they say it was never dark in the Doeff Room. All because of that one book, can you imagine? So that gives you an idea of the impact that Doeff had on Japan, but to think that the man himself was just a trader …

Keene   A trader, yes. I saw a Dutch–Japanese dictionary on display at Tsuwano, but only one. I was surprised by the richness of the example sentences it contained. It was quite well made. I don't think there are

108   Chapter 6

many dictionaries even today with so many usage examples. And it was handwritten, no less. The quality of the handwriting was amazing too. Not many people can write Roman letters by hand so nicely these days.

Philipp Franz von Siebold

Shiba   As you say, the Dutch at Dejima were traders. But around the time that Philipp Franz von Siebold (1796–1866) arrived, academics in Europe and America were starting to take an active interest in the many fascinating plants and minerals of Asia. They seem to have been in an ongoing contest over who could bring specimens back and publish something about them first. Missionaries were conducting a lot of this work in China, but Siebold learned about a country called Japan even further to the east. He was what we would call German these days, but if I recall correctly he had some relative who was the royal doctor to the Dutch king, and through that connection had joined the Dutch navy as a ship's surgeon or something like that, and that's how he ended up in Japan. He came in pursuit of adventure, and while, as you said, most Dutch of the time weren't even interested in the Suwa Festival, Siebold was the first person to take an interest in—what to call it—I guess the cultural anthropology of Japan, in modern terms.

At the time there was a government position for official interpreter at Nagasaki, right? This person interpreted Dutch in service to the Tokugawa shogunate, and the position was passed on from generation to generation, so whoever held it probably spoke relatively good Dutch. So when the interpreter at the time met Siebold, he eventually noticed that his Dutch was a bit off. Which maybe isn't surprising, since he was German, and while he may have known some Dutch he probably wasn't fluent in it. But if anyone had found out that he was German it would have caused a huge uproar, because only the Dutch were allowed in Japan at the time. So anyway the official interpreter goes to Siebold and says, "Your Dutch sounds a bit peculiar to me," because he wants to know if the Dutch he had learned was perhaps mistaken somehow. Thinking quickly, Siebold says, "There's a dialect called High Dutch. That's what I speak." Well played, Siebold! [Laughs]

Keene Especially since the Netherlands has no highlands whatsoever. [Laughs] I'm sure Siebold had various reasons for coming to Japan, but one was that the Netherlands had long been controlled by Spain as a result of war. Doeff spent over a decade in Nagasaki, and by the end his clothing was becoming tattered, and the Japanese had started turning away from the Netherlands. I think the Dutch wanted to do something to show that the Netherlands was still a strong country, a country to be respected. As part of that, they sent an elephant to Japan, along with various other curiosities. If the situation hadn't come to that, I don't think they would have sent a scholar of Siebold's stature.

Shiba Right. Siebold had already started making quite a name for himself back in Europe, hadn't he. He was from a scholarly family of mostly university professors. Coming to a place as far away as Japan must have been quite an adventure for him. I also find it very appealing that Siebold developed such a close relationship with the Japanese students who came seeking him out.

Keene And it's quite unique that he was able to teach them not at Dejima, but in the city of Nagasaki. Technically that was a violation of the laws of the time, and there's no way the local magistrate could have ignored those rules. Siebold must have been quite an appealing figure, to get special permission to build schools and trade houses and such in Nagasaki, where it would be easier for people to visit than Dejima.

Shiba Indeed, some shogunate official must have been quite fond of him, to turn a blind eye to his coming to town. He had a good deal of freedom, relatively speaking. At Narutaki he built what was supposed

110   Chapter 6

to be a small medical school. It was little more than a shack, but as it developed into the Narutaki Academy lots of sick people got the idea that just having their pulse taken by him would cure them, so everyone started going. He kindly saw to everyone who came to him, so he was very highly regarded.

Keene   But he made one big mistake: he put his trust in Mamiya Rinzo (1780–1844)[19]. To think of how many more people he could have helped if he hadn't done that... Siebold highly respected Mamiya's work, and sent him a gift and a letter. Mamiya turned around and handed that in to the magistrate's office, which resulted in people like Takahashi Kageyasu (1785–1829), a serious scholar who was court astronomer and record keeper, being arrested and dying of illness in prison.[20] All the maps Takahashi had sent Siebold were confiscated, and Siebold himself and many of his friends were repeatedly interrogated under what could almost be called torture.

Shiba   Mamiya Rinzo was quite the wicked spy. Back when I was in elementary school he was described in our textbooks as the great man who discovered the Mamiya [Tartar] Strait, but I imagine they don't teach about him these days. Nowadays he's better known as a Tokugawa spy.

When Siebold returned to Japan[21] the daughter (Ine) he'd had there had grown up, lovingly raised by his students. They also taught her the Dutch medicine they were studying. When Siebold and his daughter were reunited, he told her she had the refined expression of a person who had studied medicine. But he must have been quite disappointed

---

19. An explorer and spy for the Tokugawa shogunate, most noted for his exploration of Sakhalin Island.
20. Takahashi had secretly sent Siebold maps of Japan, which was considered an act of espionage under shogunate law.
21. He had been expelled from Japan in 1829 as a result of the Mamiya affair, but returned in 1859 after the shogunate lifted his banishment.

by developments in Japan. The Japanese were already growing tired of the Netherlands by then, having realized that England, America, and France were much bigger countries. He tried to rebrand himself as Bavarian, but the Japanese had never heard of the place. I suppose it wouldn't have even helped if he'd gone ahead and called himself German. In any case, he must have been quite disconsolate when he returned from that second visit.

Keene   I've heard that's what happened. I can't quite remember if this was on his first visit or his second, but he once saw the bunraku puppet play *Imoseyama Onna Teikin* (The Teachings for Women) in Osaka, and was very impressed by it. When he returned to Europe he related a summary of the plot to Giacomo Meyerbeer (1791–1864), an opera composer who was very popular in France at the time. Meyerbeer found it interesting too, and said he would love to make an opera out of it, which he planned to call *The Blind Emperor*. The mountain scene in *The Teachings for Women* is quite famous, but I was never sure where the "blind emperor" bit came from. I recently got to see a performance of the whole thing at the National Theatre of Japan, and indeed there is a blind emperor at the beginning, which finally solved that mystery.

Siebold was German, but he lived in France for a long time, and while the Meyerbeer opera was never realized, the French novelist Alphonse Daudet (1840–1897) later heard about it. He sought out Siebold, apparently wanting to hear the story in detail. Siebold was living in southern Germany at the time, and Daudet made the journey all the way to his home. But when he knocked on the front door, there was no answer, no matter how long he waited. Letting himself in, he found Siebold there, dead. Daudet gives a very interesting depiction of this in his *Les Contes du lundi* (Monday Tales).

Shiba   What a romantic tale.

112   Chapter 6

Keene   A very unusual one. To think, with a slight rearrangement of
fate we might have an operatic version of *The Teachings for Women.*

J. L. C. Pompe van Meerdervoort

Shiba   Siebold was quite well received as an erudite scholar when he
returned to his home country. Meanwhile, in 1857, a doctor named
Pompe (1829–1908) had arrived in Japan. Unlike Siebold, Pompe was
the first professor of medicine to be officially invited by the Tokugawa
shogunate. Japan was still operating under an isolationist policy, but
the Ansei Treaties had been established, so Pompe wasn't quite as
restricted as Siebold had been. His arrival was quite a big deal, and
he ended up laying the foundations for modern medicine in Japan.
Siebold too taught medicine, but he didn't have the materials he needed
to teach it systematically, or enough books to teach full courses. Also,
if he taught too openly he would have been reprimanded by the shogunate, so while he had many students, everything was done in secret.
They weren't technically allowed to have direct contact with Siebold,
which meant that all of their dealings with him relied on the powers
that be turning a blind eye.

For Pompe, who was there officially, things were very different.
Well, it was all official, but the shogunate was an odd thing back then.
The government had signed the Ansei Treaties, but on the surface it
was still following an isolationist policy, so only Matsumoto Ryojun
(1832–1907) was supposed to have contact with Pompe. Matsumoto
Ryojun—he later changed his name to just Jun—was physician to the
shogun, and when the shogunate was collapsing he stuck with its forces
and accompanied them at the Goryokaku fort in Hakodate, Hokkaido.
After the Meiji Restoration, he became the Surgeon General of Japan.

So officially, Pompe was to teach Matsumoto, and only Matsumoto.
But since an overwhelming number of students wanted to study under

Pompe, someone suggested that Matsumoto take notes of what he learned from Pompe, bring them back to his place, and teach the other students. By this time Matsumoto was already physician to the shogunate, however—an immediate retainer to the shogun, with quite a bit of prestige—and doing such a silly thing would have been far beneath his station. Having no other recourse, he brought with him a brilliant linguist from Edo, a man named Shiba Ryokai from Sado province[22], who came from a family of traders and farmers. Somehow, by the time he was a teenager he could already speak two or three languages, including German, despite there being no Germans in Japan at the time. So anyway, Matsumoto Ryojun would bring this eighteen- or nineteen-year-old kid with him as his secretary, and the boy would take notes as they listened to Pompe's lectures, writing down the Dutch in shorthand. When he returned to his lodgings, the students would make copies of what he'd written. Those were Pompe's first students. It was an odd start, but that was the beginning of the Nagasaki University School of Medicine.

Now back in the Netherlands, Pompe hadn't been anything like the scholar Siebold was, and in fact we probably shouldn't call him a scholar at all. This is a bit of a side note, but during wars in Japan there was always a need to rapidly train medical officers, so the government would open provisional medical schools. Following four years of junior high school, students would study at these schools for four more years, after which they would be doctors. Even today there are practicing physicians who got their training at these provisional schools. They did the same thing back in the Netherlands, because it was probably hard to get doctors out to Batavia and places like that. Nobody wanted to be assigned to such remote, barbaric lands. I don't know how many medical schools the Netherlands had back then, but there were also these

---

22. Modern-day Niigata prefecture.

114   Chapter 6

special quick courses that one could go through on the promise of becoming a naval medical officer. That's the kind of place that Pompe graduated from, and he taught in Japan from the notes he took there. So he taught this quickie course in Western medicine to Matsumoto Ryojun, which Shiba Ryokai transcribed in shorthand, and that in turn was copied by the students waiting back at his lodgings—quite an interesting propagation of knowledge!

One of those indirect students of Pompe's was a youth named Arase. He was the son of a doctor in Mitajiri, a town in Suo province[23], and like the other students he considered Pompe to be something of a god. I mean that literally—he had such high regard for Pompe that after he became a doctor he said he owed everything to Pompe, and actually created a shrine dedicated to him, the Pompe Shrine, at his mansion in Mitajiri. [Laughs] Everyone in his family had to go pay their respects first thing in the morning.

Pompe wasn't in Japan all that long—he returned to the Netherlands after just a few years, where he remained virtually unknown. Of course, he lives on in the Pompe Shrine at the Arase residence. Arase's grandson is now honorary head of the national hospital at Zentsuji in Kagawa prefecture. This grandson wanted to translate the journal Pompe kept while in Japan, but he didn't know Dutch. There was a small private junior college in Zentsuji called Shikoku Gakuin, however, and that college had a Dutch dictionary in its library. I suppose Arase knew enough German to make sense of it, and using that dictionary alone he recently managed to get out a translation of Pompe's *Five Years in Japan*.

Pompe was certainly a kind man. He was a unique presence in Nagasaki, and acted as if his duty was to be kind to any Japanese who came to him asking to study medicine, like that was the only way he could

---

23. Modern-day eastern Yamaguchi prefecture.

justify his presence there. So he was exceedingly kind to everyone. Even now some people remain very grateful to him, to the point where one hundred years later, that grandson or great-grandson I mentioned, Arase Susumu, started studying Dutch in his fifties just to translate Pompe's writings. Pretty amazing. When I hear stories like that, I get the feeling that the relationship between Japan and the Netherlands is still alive.

William S. Clark and Lafcadio Hearn

Keene Sometimes it's difficult for us Westerners to fathom exactly why certain other Westerners became famous for what they did in Japan. Some live in Japan for many years and do various things for the Japanese, yet remain virtually unknown. On the other hand, there are those like William S. Clark (1826–1886), who became so famous in Hokkaido that even today there's a Clark Building at Hokkaido University, and one of his quotes, "Boys, be ambitious!" has practically become a proverb in Japan. But how long was he actually here? I think it was less than a year, when he was invited by the Minister of Hokkaido Development in 1876. So I question how much he was able to actually accomplish, despite his fame.

I also recently visited Matsue, in Shimane prefecture, where a grave for the famous Lafcadio Hearn (1850–1904) is located. It's a very Japanese gravesite, in a very Japanese graveyard, under which a lock of his hair is said to be carefully interred. When I read a pamphlet about the literature of Matsue, his works were listed as the city's most important and famous titles. There wasn't a single work by a Japanese author on the list. So I got curious about how much time he actually spent in Matsue, and found out it was just one year and three months. That's it. Somehow he became Matsue's most prominent literary figure in that short period of time. I find that highly ironic.

116   Chapter 6

There was a Portuguese man named Wenceslau de Moraes (1854–1929)[24] in Tokushima who also left behind writings, although most people have never heard of him. I believe his *O Bon-odori em Tokushima* (The Bon-odori in Tokushima) is one of the greatest literary works from Tokushima.

Shiba   It's an excellent book. I don't know anything better.

Keene   So some foreigners became famous after very brief stays, but then there were people like Pompe, who stayed for five years and yet is unknown to most Japanese.

Shiba   That's true, few know of Pompe. I understand that the year he passed away he was working for the Red Cross. There was an international conference for the Red Cross or something like that in Europe, and for some reason, I couldn't tell you why, Mori Ogai went to represent Japan. He'd heard that Pompe would be there, so he searched for him and found him. Ogai told him—and this might have been distorted over the years—but he told him something like, "There are those in Japan who treat you as a god," to which Pompe replied, "Those were the best years of my life." I may not be remembering it quite right, but I believe I read something to that effect in Ogai's writings.

Keene   It sounds quite plausible. Apparently Frank Lloyd Wright, the American architect who designed the previous Imperial Hotel in Tokyo, also had special feelings for Japan. Just recently a book of ukiyo-e woodblock prints he collected here was published. None of them are particularly interesting or unusual, but it's clear how important those prints were to him, and the extent to which his experiences in Japan impacted his life.

---

24. Moraes first arrived in Japan in 1889. He became consul at the Portuguese Consulate in Kobe and married a Japanese woman. He died in Tokushima in 1929.

Ernest Mason Satow

Shiba   While he isn't a literary or a cultural figure, Ernest Satow (1843–1929) certainly deserves mention as a political figure. I've told three different students heading off to study in England that Satow is the only person worth focusing their research on, but unfortunately none of them took my advice. Recently the historian Hagihara Nobutoshi (1926–2001) went over there and did extensive research. Now Ernest Satow, that's a man deserving of respect. I'd say he even changed the course of the late Tokugawa shogunate. He certainly laid down the course for the government to take, and put it back on track when it started to deviate. He was the son of a merchant, not nobility, so he didn't go to Cambridge but rather to the University of London or somewhere like that. He started working for the Consular Service as an interpreter, and when he said he wanted to learn Japanese he was told to go straight to Japan because there were no schools for that. He didn't know any Chinese when he left (in 1862), but he stopped in China long enough to pick up some Chinese, then came to the consulate in Yokohama. After just a year or two there he'd learned enough Japanese to write letters in the classical style.

Now the shogunate at that time had a thing for France. France was everywhere—it was the train that Japan hopped onto after the Netherlands. People heard that this guy Napoleon was from there, so they figured it was the strongest country in the world. The shogunate even tried to model its army after France's. Duchesne (1817–1881) was the first French ambassador, followed by Roches (1809–1901), and both were quite able leaders. Roches in particular was a very slippery diplomat who presented himself as Napoleon III's right-hand man. If you think of the two main approaches to diplomacy as the orthodox path of openness and honesty versus the path of pretense and posturing, well, Roches was in the latter camp. Nevertheless, when he arrived in Japan he stated that the current situation just would not do, and

118   Chapter 6

started behaving with a certain kind of monarchical loyalism that exceeded that of even most Japanese. His thinking was very much centered around the shogunate, though—he was quite close with them. He had only a few direct audiences with the shogun, but he talked to the shogun's inner circle about setting up a prefectural system centered around the Tokugawa clan, with the Tokugawa serving as something like presidents. I'm not exactly sure how a hereditary presidency would work, but he brought up the example of Napoleon III, how he was Napoleon's nephew and through various trials and travails became his successor, and told the Tokugawa they should do the same. That would allow them to quell their opponents in Kyoto and maintain their position for generations, he said. One man who took him to heart was [the Tokugawa statesman] Oguri Kozukenosuke (1827–1868). Oguri didn't speak any French, and probably was turned on to Roche's ideas by Kurimoto Joun (1822–1897), a brave leader and a Francophile who did speak French. So you have the French ambassador teaching the shogunate international politics and setting up plans for a redesign of Japan.

I think this was all an earnest attempt at positive change. I mean, if you go to a place you know nothing about and do your best to teach the people there something, then in a sense that's a very selfless task, in that you're trying to do more for the people than they can do for themselves. I think Roche was doing what he thought best.

Now Ernest Satow on the other hand, this twenty-two-, twenty-three-year-old guy in Yokohama, had serious doubts about what France was up to. He felt that the biggest barrier to Japan's advancement onto the international stage was its system of feudal domains, and the first step in getting rid of that was to abolish the shogunate. In his eyes feudalism just didn't have a place in modern international society. He even realized that power would need to be centralized, but not in Edo. If the new system was established with Kyoto at its core, then even farmers and townsfolk would be direct subjects of the emperor, which would mean the end of the Edo-style caste system.

In other words, Satow was one of the first people to think of the shogun as something other than the de facto emperor. International law had up to that point always treated the shogun as the emperor, even calling him that on official documents, but actually he was just the most powerful daimyo—a keen observation for some guy in his early twenties. I'm not sure if many Japanese at the time realized it. Grasping the situation from the outside may have been easier, but the fact that Satow could read documents in Japanese was also a significant factor. His knowledge of the language was so extensive that he was the only foreign ambassador to figure out the proper form of address to use when writing to government ministers, for instance. That linguistic knowledge gave him extraordinary insight into the culture.

In 1866 Satow published his vision for the future of Japan in the *Japan Times*, then a weekly newspaper printed in Yokohama. There were no copyright laws or anything back then, so somebody translated it into Japanese under the title *Eikoku Sakuron* (British Policy) and distributed a few thousand copies. One ended up in the hands of Saigo Takamori (1828–1877)[25], who read it with great interest and adopted it as his own vision. So this essay about England's vision for Japan was the thing that everyone would refer back to in discussions, and ultimately it formed the model for the Meiji Restoration. I don't think Satow was even twenty-five when he wrote it. One of his parents was Swedish, right? Satow doesn't sound like an Anglo-Saxon name to me...

Keene It's not a common name, no.

Shiba Even so, I know he was born in London. When he eventually became the British envoy to Meiji Japan [in 1895], he was granted the title "Sir," which I guess shows that England recognized his

---

25. A samurai who played an influential role in the establishment of the Meiji Restoration.

120   Chapter 6

achievements in the Far East. I wish the Japanese would do the same.

Ernest Fenollosa, Basil Hall Chamberlain, and George Bailey Sansom

Shiba   Satow later returned to England, where I understand he didn't talk much about Japan. He didn't write nostalgically about Japan, and he seems to have read mostly classical, orthodox European works. Of course, I'm just repeating Hagihara's interpretation of what he learned in England, so some information may have been lost along the way ...

But I think the reason for this is that Satow had such huge plans for Japan. He saw the Meiji Restoration as his own creation. There's no doubt he was an imperial loyalist rivaling even Saigo Takamori, but once the Meiji Restoration took place, the government ministers didn't need him any more. I think that angered him, and I understand the feeling. It's like, where's the thanks I'm owed? After all, he cared more about Japan than many of them did. I think a lot of the officials in the new Meiji government didn't realize what an important role he'd played. Besides that, he tried to do something similar when he was made High Commissioner to China following the Boxer Rebellion. He'd succeeded once, so he thought he could do it again. But China was a very large and complex nation, and his stint as the British Minister in Peking doesn't appear to have gone so well.

Probably another factor was that he had some pathological characteristics common to geniuses. This is just my personal take on things, but you know how some people have a kind of split personality, where they'll be fervently involved in some task for a while, then they'll burn out and lose all interest? I think there may have been some of that.

Keene   I think you can see that in most of the Westerners who came to Japan—it's nothing unique to Satow. For example Ernest Fenollosa (1853–1908)[26] was like that, as was Basil Hall Chamberlain (1850–

1935)[27]. I think the reason is pretty much the same in most cases. They all come to Japan and do some marvelous work that gains them great respect among the Japanese. But then they pick up student followers, and after a time those students learn how to continue the work on their own, so the teacher is no longer needed.

That was clearly the case for Fenollosa. When he first arrived in Japan, the country was selling off its national treasures. The grandfather of a close friend of mine came to Kyoto as a missionary in 1872 and was approached by a monk from the Chion-in temple who said, "We have this big bell we'd like to sell. Are you interested?" He was talking about the famous bell at that temple, which was later designated a national cultural asset. Apparently my friend's grandfather said, "Well, it's quite a splendid bell, but it's too big for my home." [Laughs] There wasn't much appreciation for Japanese antiquities back then. In that era everyone was in love with new things from the West. Fenollosa wanted to teach the Japanese the value of their old artwork. I believe that's why he took on students, Okakura Tenshin (1862–1913) foremost among them. Fenollosa returned to the United States at one point to take care of some business, but when he came back to Japan he was unable to find employment—there were already Japanese people who could do the job, so paying the high salaries that "*oyatoi gaijin*" [28] demanded was no longer necessary.

In the case of Chamberlain, he was the first professor of Japanese at the University of Tokyo, but after a while there were Japanese who could do the same job even better than he could. This seems to have disheartened him, and he spent his later years studying French literature instead. The last book he wrote was about beautiful French poetry

---

26. A professor of political economy and philosophy at the Tokyo Imperial University and noted expert on Japanese art who first came to Japan in 1878.
27. A professor of Japanese at the Tokyo Imperial University who first came to Japan in 1873.
28. Westerners in the employment of the government.

and its research. He was living in Geneva and apparently not thinking about Japan at all. It's hard to believe, but things like that happen, even to people in more common circumstances than Fenollosa and Chamberlain. When they're young they come here and attain great success, but later on life in Japan becomes trying, despite their fame. No matter how hard they study, they find themselves unable to establish a significant standing. I wonder if things weren't the same for Satow. Of course he continued his work as a diplomat, but he never again quite became the rising star he was in his youth.

Another thing that puzzles me is why a scholar as well versed in Japan as Arthur Waley (1889–1966)—the famous *Tale of Genji* translator, who unfortunately passed away a few years ago—never once in his life visited Japan. There are various theories about this, but according to one person who asked Waley directly, he said, "I have no interest in the Japan of today. Rather than see what Japan has become, I would rather spend time in its old books." Perhaps he really felt that way, but another possibility is that he was afraid of becoming disillusioned, like Chamberlain and Satow and Fenollosa had.

You see, no matter how much they did for Japan, and no matter how many followers they had here, in the end they were never able to become Japanese themselves. It's not unusual for a young British person—or French or German or what have you—to move to the United States, and after working in that country for a time, to become American. But that almost never happens in Japan. The best example, I suppose, is Lafcadio Hearn, who became a Japanese citizen and renamed himself Koizumi Yakumo, only to have his salary cut in half. He must have been surprised by the reality of no longer being treated as a foreigner. I think this experience was particularly common in the Meiji period. Japanese people at the time lacked knowledge about international politics and diplomacy, as well as things like how to handle foreign artwork, so even inexperienced Westerners could come and

teach. Fenollosa certainly isn't respected in the United States as a philosopher, and he's completely unknown as an art historian. But even
so, he was the person who introduced Hegel to the Japanese, and as a
kind of personal project, he also introduced all sorts of people to Japanese art. That's quite an accomplishment, but it's not even conceivable
today. There isn't really anything left for Westerners to come to Japan
and teach the basics of, however brilliant they may be.

Shiba   The Japanese know Chamberlain the politician, but they've by
and large forgotten Chamberlain the professor of Japanese. And yet,
the School of Linguistics at Tokyo University still teaches that the origins of the Japanese language lie in the north, which is left over from
him. So it's interesting that while his academic legacy lives on, the contributions of the man himself are largely forgotten.

Keene   Most of the British consuls have been quite accomplished men,
starting with the very first, Rutherford Alcock (1809–1897). They've
produced a great deal of solid research regarding Japan. As you mentioned before, Roche from France was another great man, but I don't
know the names of any of the American consuls or ambassadors since
Townsend Harris (1804–1878)[29]. In fact, I don't think anyone associated with the U.S. Consulate here is well known. It's the same for the
Netherlands, and Germany too. But so many of the British here were
exceptional people.

Sir George Sansom, whom I studied under at Columbia University,
had great respect for Chamberlain. Sansom first went to Japan [in
1906] as part of the British legation when he was young, and he met
Chamberlain there. The first place Sansom visited after being posted
to Japan was Hokkaido, where he translated *Tsurezuregusa* (Essays in

---

29. Negotiator of the Harris Treaty to open Japan to foreign trade and first U.S. Consul to
    Japan.

Idleness). There weren't any Japanese–English dictionaries worthy of the name back then, so I hear he had quite a hard time of it. He told me that after that he took to translating noh works like *Funa Benkei* (Benkei Aboard Ship). But Sansom was actually a historian, not a literary scholar. He's written various wonderful books, like *Japan: A Short Cultural History* and *An Historical Grammar of Japanese.* I once asked him straight out how he found the time to do all this, despite being in Japan as a diplomat. He fondly recalled the good old days, saying, "Well, at the time we had almost nothing to do. A boat would come in from England maybe once a month, which would keep us busy for a few days, but other than that we had no duties." Everyone had his own way of passing the time, and for Sansom it was taking walks. He walked all over Japan, he said. I once asked him what his most memorable experience of Japan was, and he said that once while walking in the mountains of the Kansai region he fell in with a group of bandits. Can you believe there were still folk like that back then? Apparently he became good friends with them, and they never failed to send him a New Year's card.

Shiba   Ah, the bandits of the good old days. [Laughs]

CHAPTER 7
Japanese Morals, Revisited

Furyu

Shiba   So we've discussed various topics, and looking back, one that left an especially strong impression and was particularly interesting to me was your take on Ashikaga Yoshimasa (1436–1490). I think you called him something like a worthless politician. When I stop to think about it that's exactly what he was, but we Japanese don't really expect shoguns to have political skills in the first place. That was true in Yoshimasa's days as well as now. In fact, most people would probably say that shoguns lack political skills practically by definition, and they certainly wouldn't go on about their sense of political morality. That's what makes your negative appraisal of him so interesting. It got me thinking about a separate question, namely, where do politicians like Yoshimasa get their attitudes? I suppose it's a matter of *furyu*[1]. He seems to have found value in life only through furyu, not by governing for the people or living his life for them. Back in the Kamakura period, three generations of the Hojo clan[2] did their best to rule well, despite their lack of formal education. They were good rulers, the kind they sing about in *Hachinoki* (The Potted Tree)[3], but when we get to the

---

1. *Furyu* is the aesthetic of refined tastes and manners expected in a sophisticated person, particularly with regard to appreciation of arts, literature, fashion, and natural scenery. The concept first arrived in Japan from China around the eighth century, and took on various connotations in different eras.
2. Hojo Tokimasa (1138-1215), Hojo Yoshitoki (1163-1224), Hojo Yasutoki (1183-1242) regents in name but de facto rulers during the Kamakura shogunate.

126　　Chapter 7

highly refined rulers of the Ashikaga shogunate everything is about furyu. They seek value only in furyu, but nobody seems to criticize them for it.

Keene　As we discussed earlier, though, that wasn't quite true in [his grandfather] Yoshimitsu's time.

Shiba　Yoshimitsu at least showed some initiative.

Keene　Sure, he unified the country and achieved various other things by virtue of his own efforts. Of course, even in terms of furyu, he was a match for Yoshimasa. He was quite an expert on noh drama, so much so that even Zeami (see pg. 52) commented that there was likely no one else with a higher appreciation for it. He was a very clever politician as well. His correspondence with mainland China was very skillfully written.

Shiba　Your impressions of all this are original, and very interesting. At the end of the Tokugawa shogunate, Sakamoto Ryoma asked Katsu Kaishu, "Just what kind of country is the United States?" Katsu wasn't sure how to answer succinctly, so he just said, "The President of the United States was worried as to whether his maids were being paid enough." This surprised Sakamoto to no end, since no shogun of Japan would concern himself with such a thing. He said this was one of the things that convinced him the Tokugawa must be removed from power and enamored him with the U.S. system of government. We Japanese consider Ashikaga Yoshimasa to be a very prominent figure, responsible for creating the Higashiyama culture, but you're able to look at him as a president and say, "He wasn't all that good." That's quite interesting. But I'd like to discuss this topic of furyu a bit more…

---

3. A song from noh drama relating a legend about Hojo Tokiyori (1227–1263), who rewards a poor retired warrior for his kindness to the ruler when he is disguised as a traveling monk.

Going way back to when the [Korean] kingdom of Paekche fell [in 660], which was around the time the Asuka culture was developing in Japan, the last king of Paekche was a good, well-regarded ruler at first, but from middle age on he spent his life pursuing sensual pleasures. As to why he changed so dramatically, well, Silla was allied with the Tang dynasty and so was a little different, but the Paekche culture was basically the Six Dynasties (220–589) culture of mainland China from the Yangtze river south, right? I think that culture had a profound effect on the Paekche king.

Specifically, as you know, during the Six Dynasties era the Han Chinese were expelled from northern China and migrated south of the Yangtze. Once there, they developed something like a nobility for the first time in Chinese history. That nobility didn't engage in politics—politics was considered extremely unsophisticated, as was warfare—but rather placed value in furyu, and concerned themselves only with its enjoyment. They also considered Confucianism unsophisticated, a kind of ideology for the common folk. They were more interested in the older teachings of people like Laozi and Zhuang Zhou, and in Buddhism. Not to imply that those are depraved teachings, but the Six Kingdoms era was one of extreme decadence, and there are traces of that very same culture being imported into Paekche.

So I think the last king of Paekche spent his later years pursuing a Six Kingdoms lifestyle. Yoshimasa's era was still far in the future, but his grandfather Yoshimitsu engaged in extensive trade with areas south of the Yangtze, where the unique values of furyu took root. Sometimes I wonder if Yoshimasa was influenced by that, but then I turn around and think that it's ridiculous and try to defend him.

Keene   I'm sure he's smiling at your words from his place in hell, since I'm sure that's where he must be now. [Laughs] When we were at Ginkakuji temple earlier I learned that Yoshimasa is praised as the first

128   Chapter 7

person to design a four-and-a-half-tatami-mat room[4], which helped me realize just how much value the Japanese place on aesthetics.

Shiba   Yes, we tend to value aesthetic heroes over political justice. We don't look to them for salvation, we just think they're classy because they were very refined and could build great tea rooms.

Keene   Looking at it another way, the three generations of the Hojo clan that served as regent governed honestly and dedicated their lives to the nation of Japan, but they aren't popular at all.

Shiba   That's right. These days we think of them as kind of bleak and almost barbaric, so no, they aren't popular. Then again, I couldn't say why we feel fondness for a wastrel like Yoshimasa. Actually, I'd like to ask why you think that is.

Keene   Well, the Japanese even today are quite indulgent of artists. An artist who produces high-quality work tends to be forgiven for whatever personal peccadillos they might have. Don't you agree? I don't think that's quite the case in China. If you ask the Chinese what makes Du Fu a great poet, they'll say it's because he worked so hard for his country, or because he was so troubled by the barbarian incursions, things like that. But you'd never hear a Japanese person say something like that. Ask a Japanese what's so great about Fujiwara no Teika (1162–1241), and they'll say something about the beauty and profundity of his tanka poems. But Teika didn't consider the war of his day[5] to have anything to do with him—in his diary *Meigetsuki* he wrote, "Banners and armies are nothing to me." The Chinese would consider that a very poor attitude—they would say that the fate of your country in war is of ultimate concern, even if you're an aristocrat or a great

---

4. The size of traditional Japanese rooms is measured in the number of tatami mats required to floor it.
5. The Jokyu War (1221) between the Hojo clan and the retired emperor Go-Toba.

artist. But the Japanese don't mind an irresponsible outlook, so long as your art is good.

Shiba   Yes, that's a big difference between Japan and China. As to where it comes from, well, I suppose the answer lies in conditions unique to Japan. But to give a similar example at least—I believe from the Six Dynasties period (222–589), the capital was in an area south of the Yangtze river that in modern times produced many Chinese revolutionaries—that was an area where for a long time the Confucianism was quite different, right? The Confucianism to the north was all about proper government, but as you head south you get this kind of degenerate Confucianism that's about enjoyment for the warrior class. [Chinese historian] Kaizuka Shigeki wrote somewhere that, "Chinese officials had split personalities. They would engage in proper Confucianism while they were in government offices, but upon returning home they reverted to Laozi and Zhuang Zhou." I think that kind of thing started in the Six Dynasties period, and at some point the peculiar tendency to place ultimate value in the pursuit of furyu made its way into Japan ...

Keene   Actually in China I think it might have come a little later, in the Song dynasty (960–1279), especially the Southern Song dynasty (1127–1279). For a long time the Japanese called Chinese literati paintings "Southern School" works, which I believe shows that Southern Song culture had the most powerful effect on Japan. The poetry of that time is a good fit for Japan too. It's emotional, and doesn't often take up grandiose themes. The poems tend to be about things like the sorrows of aging and how one's life seems like a candle that's burning down. Easy concepts for the Japanese to grasp, written in an emotive style. More than the "greats" like Du Fu, I think they preferred more down-to-earth, relatable poets like Li He (791–817). In any case, the aesthetics of the Song era had a profound effect on Japan.

130   Chapter 7

Shiba   Without a doubt.

Keene   I think that's even true for waka poems, especially those in the style of Kyogoku (1254–1332) and Reizei (949–1011), which show a significant influence. You could probably argue that all this extends even to Fujiwara no Teika, and to other arts like painting and pottery. Currently Tang-era works are popular, especially sancai ceramics, but for many years Song porcelains and celadon were most highly valued. Not to imply that the Chinese hate the Song era, but I think most prefer the Tang. I don't think there are many Song fans out there.

Shiba   I can see how the Song era, especially that of the Southern Song, is a good fit with the Japanese. When the *wako* pirates headed there, they were after calligraphy and paintings. The Chinese knew that, so they sold them to anyone who showed up. All fakes, though. [Laughs] So maybe we were unknowingly affected by the fake artwork of Southern China.

Keene   But even considering the real stuff we see examples like the artwork of Muqi Fachang (1210?–1269?), which is popular in Japan but virtually unknown in China. The West largely came to know Chinese artwork via Japan, so the view of Chinese art there is very similar to Japan's. Well, that's less true today, but still ... The Chinese artwork that was preserved in Japan was for many years considered in the West to be the best Chinese art. Part of that is due to Fenollosa. He produced a massive two-volume work called *Epochs of Chinese and Japanese Art*, in which you can see that his personal preferences were very close to those of the Japanese.

Shiba   I see, very interesting. A Tang-era favorite among the Japanese is Emperor Xuanzong (685–762), whose rule brought about the end of that dynasty. His love for his consort Yang Guifei (719–756) led him to ignore his official duties, to the point that An Lushan (703–757) chased him out of office. So I suppose Xuanzong was the Chinese equivalent of Ashikaga Yoshimasa. I don't think the Japanese started thinking about politics in terms of "good politicians" that they could entrust the country to until around the end of the Tokugawa shogunate, heading into the Meiji Restoration. Before that, good governance wasn't necessarily sufficient to warrant praise.

A Country Without Heroes

Keene   How do you think most Japanese would answer if they were asked to name the greatest person in Japanese history?

Shiba   Well there's an interesting question. I wonder who everyone could agree upon. Minamoto no Yoritomo (1147–1199)[6] was a good ruler, but he isn't popular. Minamoto no Yoshitsune (1159–1189)[7] is popular, but he was a fool. Moving ahead to the Meiji Restoration, Okubo Toshimichi (1830–1878) was an excellent statesman, and I consider him a great man, but that spoiled brat Saigo Takamori (1828–1877) is infinitely more beloved.

Keene   Even when I myself read Japanese history, I'm most attracted to politicians who are a little bit—how to put this—irresponsible, I suppose. People like the very reckless Taira no Kiyomori (1118–1181)[8], or Toyotomi Hideyoshi (1536–1598)[9]. It's highly questionable whether those men were great politicians, but if you study Japanese history it's hard to forget someone like Kiyomori, even if [his eldest son] Shigemori (1138–1179) was the better person.

---

6. First shogun of the Kamakura shogunate.
7. A Minamoto clan samurai and younger brother of Yoritomo.
8. Military leader and grandfather of the Emperor Antoku, who took the throne after Kiyomori staged a coup d'état against the reigning Emperor Takakura.
9. The successor of Oda Nobunaga who ended the Warring States period by unifying Japan.

132   Chapter 7

Shiba   I wonder if it's because politics is a highly masculine activity, but we Japanese have difficulty viewing it that way. Perhaps we see it as more feminine. Maybe Saigo Takamori is more popular than Okubo because he wrote better poetry and came up with some good lines from time to time.

Keene   Put that way, Japan is a very odd country indeed. It's a country without heroes. Pretty much every country, regardless of how insignificant, has at least one hero. But if you were to ask ten people here who they respect the most, you'd probably get ten different answers, for all kinds of reasons. I think that's quite peculiar for a country with such a long history, and that's made such great contributions to world history ... Anyway, as far as I can tell, the Japanese have different categories for leaders they respect and those whom they actually like.

Shiba   That's true. Toyotomi Hideyoshi was a strange fellow, but everyone likes him. Tokugawa Ieyasu (1543–1616)[10] built the structure of Edo government, and his successes and failures make him a preeminent politician, but he isn't popular today. If someone said you remind them of Ieyasu those would be fighting words, but if they compared you to Hideyoshi you'd be all smiles. I agree, it's weird.

Keene   Even in the Tokugawa era, for example if you were to compare the fifth shogun Tsunayoshi (1646–1709) with the eighth shogun Yoshimune (1684–1751), Yoshimune rebuilt the Japanese economy through the Kyoho Reforms and forbade luxurious lifestyles and did all of these politically ambitious things, but he's not popular at all. Meanwhile Tsunayoshi is highly regarded as a Genroku-era shogun, despite his morally questionable acts.

Shiba   Well, I don't know that people were being affectionate when they called him "the dog shogun",[11] but he does have a certain

---

10. Founder of the Tokugawa shogunate.

colorful image. But you're right, there aren't really any heroes like Hong Xiuquan (1814–1864) of the Taiping Rebellion, figures who took a stand for the people, that kind of thing. Perhaps the social foundation necessary for something like that to happen simply didn't exist.

Keene　There were very few figures like that, if any. Do you suppose, for example, that Amakusa Shiro (1621–1638) of the Shimabara Rebellion[12] earned the fame he achieved?

Shiba　I think he was a figurehead, even at the time. He's celebrated not because he was powerful, but because he was powerless. I assume he was a handsome young boy, noble and clever by anyone's standards. That made for an ideal general, but the advisors who surrounded him were responsible for all the actual operations. They needed someone like him for everyone to rally around.

Keene　I suppose you're right. So we can't really call him a hero, either.

Japanese Confucianism Revisited

Shiba　I'd like to get back to something we were discussing before, about the basis for Japanese morals, or what model they follow. You're a foremost expert on Edo-period literature, so let's view it from that perspective. You say that Japanese literature shows Confucianism extending even into the world of ordinary people, right? My definition of Confucianism may be a bit on the dogmatic side, but I see it as a social system rather than as something written in a book. I say we've never had a Confucian social structure, and while Confucianism may have served as a foundation for morality, it never extended to our daily lives or systems, and therefore its influence on Japan has always been

---

11. Tsunayoshi was given this nickname because of his many laws for the protection of dogs.
12. A failed uprising of Japanese Catholics led by Amakusa against the shogunate, which resulted in Amakusa's execution.

134   Chapter 7

relatively minor.

For example, aside from social systems, one of the more important aspects of Confucianism is its emphasis on action. By action I mean action on a grand scale, such as instigating revolution. Mencius wrote quite extensively about the behavior of kings and nobles, chastising them for thinking only of their personal gain, to the point where his writings were actually feared in Japan. There was a legend, probably from around the Heian period, that any Chinese boat with the writings of Mencius on board was sure to become shipwrecked. If you're going to follow his writings, you have to incorporate Confucianism into social systems. More specifically, you have to instigate a revolution, and that idea was not welcome in Japan. So Mencius remained largely unknown, even in the Edo period, and those who did read his works mostly considered them second- or third-rate material. The only person who extolled his virtues was the late-Tokugawa intellectual Yoshida Shoin (1830–1859), who went on and on about how great Mencius was and devoted all of his lectures to the subject. But I think he's about the only one throughout the entire Edo period. That really makes me question Confucianism's place in Japan, and the more I think about it, the more I'm convinced we weren't very affected by it.

Keene   Well, I view the culture of the Tokugawa era primarily through its literature, but reading the plays of Chikamatsu and similar works, they all seem to conform to Confucian thought in most respects. Up to a point, that is.

Shiba   I see. Well, I certainly agree with you on the "up to a point" part.

Keene   Once you go beyond that point, all sense of morality disappears. Everything goes askew. Consider Chikamatsu's play *Nebiki no Kadomatsu* (The Uprooted Pine), for example. The protagonist Yojibei is placed in a very tight spot. He loves his wife Okiku, but he's also in love with the courtesan Azuma, and he doesn't know what to do about it. They're both good, true women, and in the end the situation drives Yojibei crazy. I'm pretty sure viewers of the time felt sympathy for him, and they felt that way because Yojibei's thoughts are authentic, and his actions are all based on genuine emotions. He doesn't stop to consider what he stands to gain or lose, and he certainly isn't thinking in Confucian terms. I find that to be very Japanese. The Confucian approach, on the other hand, would be to control oneself before reaching the point of insanity.

Shiba   Yes, I agree. Confucianism provides methods for thinking about things and developing those thoughts into logic. But Confucianism has all these absolutes, right? There are certain things that are important above all others. For example, the Five Constants are absolute. But the Japanese don't treat these absolutes as the final answer. They treat them as simply the first problem.

Keene   I completely agree that they aren't considered the absolute final word, but I do think they carry people pretty far as the most important consideration in making decisions. And that point is where things become troubling. For example, say there's a man who has a powerful sense of filial duty, but one day he falls in love with a certain woman. It's an adulterous love, but even so, his emotions are so strong that he wants to be with the woman, even if doing so leads to his parents being thrown into a dungeon. Running away with the girl you love even under those conditions would require quite a bit of passion, but up to that point his ordinary life was Confucian.

Shiba   During the Edo period people frequently discussed *shonenba*—the moment of decision. I think that the Japanese have a tendency to suddenly become a different kind of person in situations like that. Not the Chinese, though. I think that lack of change is true Confucianism. In thinking about the problem of filial piety you brought up, I feel like I've gotten a much better sense of the Chinese sense of filial piety. Among Chinese people who are connected within a single village or tribe, respect for the elderly is highly valued, and filial piety is owed even to very distant relatives if they're older than you. All of this is to protect your own horizontal social structure and prevent it from collapsing. Three thousand, even five thousand years of history have shown that you can't depend on the government for help, so you have to do everything you can to keep these horizontal structures in place. Filial piety in Japan, however, is more like taking your mother out for a show because she seems to be tired recently. Things go far beyond that in China. The roots go deeper into society's core, so deep that I wonder if they form the basis from which Chinese society developed. Filial piety is something they feel down to their bones. That never quite crossed over to the Japanese.

Keene There's a very curious book by Ihara Saikaku (1642–1693) called *Honcho Niju Fuko* (Twenty Cases of Unfilial Children), which describes various people who fail at their filial duties. It makes me wonder if maybe people back then were feeling some resistance to the version of filial duty that had been imported from China. It probably just didn't work here. Even so, doesn't it seem that the Japanese considered a Confucian lifestyle to be a good way to live, by and large? Particularly during the Tokugawa shogunate, which promoted the ideals of respecting one's father at home and honoring one's feudal lord and daimyo, and on up the pyramid to the shogun at the top.

Shiba It certainly seems like the best system for preserving the Tokugawa regime.

Keene You said that the filial piety practiced here differed from that of China, but from my perspective it seems largely the same. That's especially true if you include European countries in the comparison. Even within Japan, the morality of the Muromachi era was completely different from that of Edo. The history of the Muromachi era is filled with examples of poor treatment of one's parents, to the point of murdering them.

Shiba   And things were even worse in the Kamakura period. That's definitely an era that could have used some filial piety. The nobility in Kyoto had picked up some of those Confucianism-influenced ideals as you describe them from a relatively early time, so they weren't so bad. When they saw everything that was going on in Kamakura, they considered that lot to be a horde of barbarians.

Religion and the Common People

Shiba   When I question the foundation of Japanese morals, I'm not questioning whether they're based on Confucianism or Buddhism. As I've been saying, I think Buddhism just muddied the waters of the Japanese spirit. Buddhism is largely about a way of living, which is presented in the form of strictures. Shingon Buddhism has these strictures, and so does Tendai Buddhism, and even Jodo. So these rules get passed on along with points of etiquette for daily life, but where do they come from? Well, they were meant to guide the daily life of Indian monks. But if you're going to live the life of an Indian monk you have to at least live in Indian society, you can't just bring all that and drop it on Japan. If you really want to bring Buddhism here you have to bring Indian society along with it, or move all the Japanese to India. So practicing Buddhism in Japan is like smelling the bacon but not actually eating it. For example, it's questionable whether Kamo no Chomei (1155–1216)[13] of *Hojoki* (An Account of My Hut) fame was

---

13. A poet and essayist who lived as a hermit monk.

138   Chapter 7

really a Buddhist …

Keene   Especially toward the end.

Shiba   That work is definitely situated within a Japanese poetic milieu. It's hard to imagine anything so soft coming out of the harsh conditions of India that produced the Buddha.

Keene   Indeed. But still, I think the greatest accomplishment across the long history of the Japanese people has been their skillful selection of those aspects of foreign culture best suited to Japan. Take the Japanese lifestyle of the Tokugawa era, for example. When you were born you would be taken to a Shinto shrine for presentation to the gods, and you would also have a Shinto ceremony when you got married, but you would live a predominantly Confucian life and be buried with a Buddhist ceremony. All three of those religions—well, Confucianism isn't really a religion, but still—all three are based on completely different principles. They even contradict each other. Shinto says that this world we live in is the best place there is, and that when we die we all go to a "polluted land" called *yomi*. On the other hand, Buddhism says this world is just an illusion, that *this* is the polluted land, but we'll be in a purer place after we die. Confucianism says this is it, there is no other place. [Laughs] So all three are in total contradiction. It's quite a feat to believe in all three at once.

Shiba   Well the way I see it, the Japanese are basically Shinto. I think that a very old Shinto remains within us, a Shinto from before it was even called Shinto. Various people, such as Hirata Atsutane (1776–1843), have tried to conceptualize and systematize it, and the State Shinto of the Meiji period is another example of that, but I see those as deviations from the real thing. Shinto was originally just about purifying things, such as rooms or whatever. It doesn't have doctrines or anything like them. There are just certain places where gods exist, and those are good places to, say, lay down some gravel to keep it pure. I'm not sure where this idea of purifying came from, whether it was about keeping things sanitary or something, but that's basically all there is, so it's easy to saddle Buddhism or Confucianism on top of it. This is what I meant before when I said Japan is like a big plate (see pg. 94). The Japanese have this Shintoistic space within them, and that space is sometimes filled with Buddhism and sometimes with Confucianism, but those other beliefs are always cast in a Shinto-shaped mold.

Keene   Even so, the fact remains that the love-suicide dramas of Chikamatsu captured the hearts of Japan. If the Japanese people had only Shintoistic beliefs then I don't think they would have sympathized with those stories. A couple who couldn't remain together in this world would commit suicide together because they believed they could be reunited in paradise—"reborn on the same lotus leaf in the pure lands of the West"—after death. That's not something you would read in any Shinto book.

Shiba   Definitely not.

Keene   But still this idea of being reunited in the "pure land" was very important to the Japanese of that time.

Primal Shinto

Shiba   I think even the idea that yomi, the land of the dead, is a polluted place developed later. The original Shinto just had, in a word, a "demented space." Later on, in the *Kojiki* and *Nihon Shoki*, there are tales of people going to yomi and finding it to be polluted, which got systematized into Shinto. If that were the case, simple Shinto would say you could just clean the place and purify it. But then along comes Buddhism, and by the Edo period it's penetrated deep into the lives of common people. According to that religion, after we die we can go to paradise, which allowed couples to think they could die a beautiful death and meet again on a lotus leaf somewhere. I wonder if that idea somehow made its way into Shinto, being the accommodating flat plate that it is.

Keene   I think a Buddhist would say just the opposite, that Shinto ideas made their way into Buddhism. *Ryobu* (Dual Aspect) Shinto is like that, with its tenet that the gods exist to protect the Buddha. That's how things got interpreted, and for a long time the Japanese didn't really distinguish between the two belief systems. You'd find Shinto shrines and Buddhist temples within the same precincts, and in some cases a Shinto priest would also be a Buddhist monk. I guess that made things convenient.

Shiba   Yeah, the Chinese and Koreans laugh at examples of Shinto–Buddhist syncretism like that. I suppose it's a hard concept to grasp. But it's so much a part of our lives that to me it feels like the most natural state of things. It makes me really mad to think about the people in the Meiji period who tried to separate the two.

But if you look further back in history, you see things like Buddhist monks coming and going at the sacred palace in Kyoto. The Emperor had family temples at both Mt. Hiei and Mt. Koya—the Sennyu temple, was it?—so I guess the imperial family supported both Tendai and Shingon Buddhism. If somebody in the royal family got sick they'd call a monk to perform healing rituals, but the monk wouldn't be allowed into the palace. I only realized this recently, but as followers of the Buddha monks were seen as unclean, so they weren't allowed inside. Even emperors who were devout Buddhists themselves wouldn't let monks enter the palace. Later on, in the Edo period, the palace doctors would shave their heads and dress like monks, and they weren't allowed into the emperor's chambers either. I suppose that complicated matters when the emperor got sick, but even then they couldn't enter. A concept like that could only have come from Shinto, right?

Keene   I'd say so. Another example is that although Basho wasn't a monk when he visited Ise shrine, he looked like one because he'd shaved his head, so they wouldn't let him in. That's definitely a true story, but in general everything was somewhat muddled. Hayashi Razan (1583–1657)[14] shaved his head when he gave his first lecture on Confucianism before the shogun, and it's interesting that even though he was delivering a message in stark contrast to Buddhism, he still had to present himself as a monk.

Shiba   I think Hayashi shaved his head in order to position himself outside mainstream life, which allowed him to present himself before the shogun—he wouldn't have had sufficient social rank to do so otherwise.

Keene   As an aside, there's a collection of letters written by men scheduled for execution as war criminals in 1948. These were the last letters they wrote, so I'm sure they were in a unique state of mind, but many of them mention Buddhism—almost all of them, in fact. But I don't think a single one brings up Shintoism.

Shiba   Well now that's quite interesting. But I wouldn't say that means Shinto wasn't present—Shinto is the plate, and you don't eat your plate. It's what's put on the plate that helps you.

Keene   I think it's in moments of great danger that we're most likely to start believing in things we'd previously overlooked, like the Buddha. But even when they're faced with impending execution, nobody prays to the Shinto goddess Amaterasu.

Shiba   Well that's because nobody would count on Amaterasu for

---

14. An official Confucian scholar in the Tokugawa shogunate.

help. It's not like she's going to save you from the afterlife… For better or worse, I think that's an example of Japanese opportunism. If I'm about to die, I might as well hope for Buddhahood.

CHAPTER 8
The Culture of Edo

The warrior culture of Kyoto and the townsfolk culture of Edo

Shiba   I feel bad saying this to you, Edo culture expert that you are, but as you've probably picked up in our conversations so far, to be honest I just can't bring myself to like the Edo period (1603–1868)[1]. I prefer the Warring States period—not because I like war, but because I feel that's when the Japanese represented themselves best. Take, for example, the buildings of the Edo period. They're covered in gratuitous decorations that do absolutely nothing for me. I don't like them in the same way I don't like Toshogu shrine in Nikko, which we talked about before, or the Confucian Yushima Seido temple.

Keene   Is that so? I'd always considered the Edo period to be the era that the Japanese felt the closest to—certain specialists excluded. Most period films take place during the late Edo, and very few go as far back as the Heian period (794–1185). The Meiji period (1868–1912) is still recent enough that the fashions of the time just look quaint. Toward the end of the Edo period you have all these splendid-looking samurai, but in the early Meiji, around the time the Rokumeikan hall was built, everyone is wearing this odd blend of Japanese and Western clothing that makes them look old-fashioned, so I think it's hard for the average modern Japanese to relate. That's probably why the setting for most period novels and films ends up being not the Heian or Kamakura

---

1. An alternative name for the time of the Tokugawa shogunate.

144   Chapter 8

period (1185–1333), but the Edo, particularly toward its end.

Shiba   I think it's because we have a stronger sense of the humanity of that time. But when you say Edo here, you're really talking about the Genroku period (1688–1704)[2]. If you watch films and television shows about the forty-seven ronin[3], the women in those shows should be wearing their hair in the Genroku style, but people today don't really relate to that, so they use the more familiar Takashimada style, despite its being from the late Edo. I've been told that this is done to give viewers a better sense that a beautiful woman is entering a scene. So even within the Edo period, there are periods that modern Japanese can relate to more easily.

Keene   Yes, I suppose that today the late Edo feels the most representative of the entire period. It gives people the feeling of "old Japan," and of a time when the women were very beautiful. I get the sense that even most writers who are enamored with that period tend to focus on its later years. Nagai Kafu (1879–1959) and Tanizaki Junichiro (1886–1965) are good examples. It wasn't a period of particularly remarkable cultural advancement—the architecture of that time is certainly nothing special, and neither is the literature. Nonetheless, the kabuki plays of Kawatake Mokuami (1816–1893) certainly indicate that he felt the late Edo was the true old Japan. I'm sure that the character Benten Kozo in Kawatake's *Shiranami Gonin Otoko* (Five Men of the White Waves)[4] was supposed to be an iconic representation of the Japanese of old.

Shiba   There are still people like that. Every now and then you run

---

2. The part of the Edo period during which Emperor Higashiyama reigned.

3. A series of tales related to an eighteenth-century historical event in which a band of leaderless samurai sought revenge for the death of their master.

4. A common name for *Aoto Zoshi Hana no Nishikie* (The Story of Aoto and the Gorgeous Woodblock Print).

into someone in Tokyo's *shitamachi* districts[5]—a gardener or such—and you think, "Now this is an Edo man." Someone with a personality that you won't find anywhere else in the world, one that definitely hails back to the Edo era.

Keene If you think about it, the Edo period spans 270 years, so you can't expect it to all be the same. For one thing, the culture of Kyoto and Osaka dominated the first half, while Edo culture dominated the rest. The concept of *chonin*[6] culture existed even when Kyoto was dominant, but the real cultural focus of that time was the samurai. On the other hand, Edo was ostensibly a samurai town, but still very chonin-focused.

Shiba A very interesting observation!

Keene When you see these "Edo men" you mentioned, I'll bet they're craftsmen or merchants, not people who remind you of samurai. The culture of the first half of the Edo era, including the Genroku period, was created mostly by samurai. There are important exceptions to that, like the poet Ihara Saikaku (1642–1693), but people like Chikamatsu and Basho and, going even further back, Matsunaga Teitoku (1571–1653)—they all came from samurai families. But in the latter half of the Edo era, most of the cultural figures were chonin. That's where the paradox comes from—the culture of samurai-centric Edo was largely developed by chonin for their own enjoyment.

Shiba Well that's an interesting theory to consider. But now that you mention it, even icons of chonin literature like Saikaku were extremely conscious of the samurai.

---

5. The Tokyo "low town" districts that were typically inhabited by Edo's lower classes.
6. Townsfolk, including merchants, traders, and artisans, but not farmers. The chonin rose to social prominence through the Edo era due to their economic advancement, despite their low position in the traditional social hierarchy.

146   Chapter 8

Keene   Saikaku practically worshipped them. He didn't write a single bad thing about them. It's almost like he considered the samurai to
be a separate breed of human. Stories like *Bukegiri Monogatari* (Tales
of Samurai Honor) go as far as saying that the samurai are without
fault, and that even if a samurai should find himself penniless, mar-
rying a chonin woman would doubtless result in his ruin. A samurai
should only marry the daughter of another samurai—that's definitely
the stance that Saikaku took.

The Forty-Seven Ronin

Shiba   As I mentioned earlier when we were talking about loyalty,
I don't think Japanese loyalty is based on Confucianism. Confucian
loyalty implies a certain seriousness, whereas Japanese loyalty is more
about being faithful to your master—although it does go a bit broader
and deeper than that. That second kind of loyalty was heavily promoted
in the Edo era, and in the early Edo in particular it meant loyalty to
the master as an individual. For example, take the Genroku Ako incident[7]. When one of the samurai involved in that incident introduced
himself, he would say something like, "I'm Oishi Kuranosuke, samurai of Takumi no kami[8] Asano." But you wouldn't expect someone in
the late Edo era to call himself "Katsura Kogoro, samurai of Minister
Mori." It would be "Katsura Kogoro, clansman of the Choshu domain,"
or "Saigo Takamori, clansman of the Satsuma domain." I think that
shows a remarkable change in social consciousness toward the end of
the Edo period, with people developing a clear concept of provinces as
states. Those states had lords and rulers associated with them, but they
were a more like symbols than individuals, and in a strange twist those

---

7. The incident that provoked the formation of the forty-seven ronin, described in more
   detail below.
8. "Chief Carpenter," an honorary imperial title.

The Culture of Edo   147

symbolic personages, too, were expected to show loyalty to the state. For example, even if Mori were the lord of the Choshu domain, ignoring the demands of some influential extremist group could result in his being poisoned. During the Meiji era someone once said to the former Lord Mori, "As the political situation fluctuated within your domain, you always seemed to side with the most powerful force. Why didn't you stick to your principles?" To that he replied, "Back then, principles would get you killed." In other words, the Choshu domain was a state.

So even within the Edo era, while loyalty remained an important factor throughout, it meant something very different in the early versus the late period. While it's true that the Edo period tried to fit people into a certain mold, there was a definite shift in character starting around its midpoint.

Keene   The year before last I translated a tale of the forty-seven ronin, and I started thinking about loyalty while writing the preface. In recent years Japanese scholars have been writing that Asano, the master of the forty-seven ronin, didn't deserve such adoration from his retainers—that he was a skinflint, that he was deeply in debt, and so on—while his rival Kira Yoshinaka[9] was a splendid man who implemented irrigation projects that greatly aided his farmers and so on. I'm sure these historians are writing such things in an attempt to intrigue their readers, but as I see it, if we're talking about loyalty, then the fidelity of the forty-seven ronin is all the more admirable if that was indeed the situation. I mean, it's easy to remain loyal to a wonderful boss. But remaining loyal even to a slovenly lout? That's something else entirely.

---

9. According to the forty-seven ronin stories, Kira Yoshinaka (1641–1703) publicly insulted Asano while the two were in Edo castle, provoking Asano to draw his sword and attempt to kill Kira. Drawing weapons within the castle was strictly forbidden, so Asano was sentenced to commit ritual suicide. It was for this incident that Asano's retainers sought revenge on Kira.

148   Chapter 8

Shiba   I suppose that's the nature of loyalty. I've been told that I'm related to one of the forty-seven ronin, but I have something of an aversion to that tale. I've never considered writing about it, or even thought much about it, but for some reason I still get annoyed when I hear someone praising Kira Yoshinaka. But anyway, yes, you see that kind of samurai loyalty to worthless lords like Asano in the Genroku period, but by the late Edo it's completely gone. Loyalty by then is directed toward the domain instead.

Keene   Loyalty has to be absolute, right? You can't really make merchant-like deals with it, saying, "You've done such-and-such for me, so I owe you this amount of loyalty." I think the ideal bushido warrior was one who remained absolutely loyal to his lord, no matter how that lord treated him. I'm sure that's how many people at the time thought about it. The common sense of our time makes us assume this must have been very difficult, especially if one's lord was not particularly admirable. Most of us would consider living in a feudal society to be difficult in itself, but actually, most samurai appear to have been quite content with the stipends their lords gave them. But when we consider their situation today, we wonder if it wouldn't have been preferable to be free, without a lord over us—to go where we wanted and take any job. But masterless samurai considered that a very sad situation. It didn't make them feel free at all.

Shiba   Far beyond sad—many would rather have been sent to hell. The loss of position is a terrible thing to the Japanese.

Translating Edo Literature

Keene   When I translate literature from the Edo era, I often wonder if the work I'm translating has universality. I think the most universal Edo works are the poems of Basho. Most Westerners can relate to

The Culture of Edo   149

The Narrow Road to Oku or his haiku, despite the impossibility of giving a truly faithful translation of haiku. I don't think there are many cultured Westerners who would find *The Narrow Road to Oku* uninteresting. A writer like Chikamatsu is another story, though. Appreciating his works requires a particular sense of morality and ethics, and that gets in the way of the story. It's quite unfortunate, because I think his plays would be very moving if they simply focused on human relationships. Take for example the last scene in *Shinju Ten no Amijima* (The Love Suicides at Amijima), where the lovers Jihei and Koharu go on and on about their duty to Jihei's wife, how they would fail her if they died together. Koharu proposes that she die down by the water, while Jihei goes off to kill himself up in the mountains, thus preventing people from knowing this was a love suicide. It's hard for a Western reader to follow that. Where they die doesn't seem to matter—it's still a double suicide regardless of the altitude at which their deaths occur. Focusing on that kind of surface-level, Confucian-in-the-worst-sense detail at the expense of developing the human emotions involved makes this a much less universal work.

But there's an even more fundamental problem. Most of the great works of the Heian period were written by women, right? I think works by female authors have a greater universality than those written by men. Women traditionally saw less of the outside world, so they turned inward, and the inner aspects of humanity vary less than our surroundings do. Jealousy is present in every country, as is love, and I think it's fair to say that the emotions felt by women are shared by all, regardless of where or when you live. Diaries like Murasaki Shikibu's and the *Kagero Nikki* (The Gossamer Years)[10] describe a world that's different from ours in its details, but nearly the same in its emotions. It's fine if you hate the woman who wrote *The Gossamer*

---

10. A diary from around 974 by an author known only as "the Mother of Michitsuna."

Years —there's a big difference between hating someone and not being able to understand them.

But Edo literature was dominated by men. Those men were concerned with issues occurring in their sphere—political and social questions, problems of Confucianism and such—and they acted under those influences. As a result they tend to write from perspectives very different from our modern ones, about what in many cases now seem like trivialities. But women living in palaces during the Heian period knew almost nothing of the outside world. That made them more contemplative, and led them to write about more fundamentally human topics. Edo literature is filled with things like how good the eel is at such-and-such a shop, and how this show or the other was so interesting, but today we have little interest in such things. I'm sure the length of some actor's nose was quite an interesting topic of conversation at the time, but it's meaningless today. Japan was a very closed society under the Tokugawa shogunate, so you get the feeling that the Japanese of the time were just amusing themselves by whispering secrets to each other.

Shiba   Whispering secrets to each other! What a great way to put it.

Keene   You don't see that at all in the Heian period, or in the Warring States period that you're so fond of. Things were more open. I put a lot of effort into translating Chikamatsu's work, and I think I did a decent job of it, but it would be impossible to actually perform his plays in English. The style is different, of course, but most problematic is the sense of morality, which is peculiar to the Edo period. I'd say another problem is their lack of dimension. It's hard to differentiate between the male protagonists in his plays. They're all handsome in the same way, and while the details of their circumstances differ, they all do pretty much the same thing. But—while Shakespeare is admittedly an exceptional case—who could fail to distinguish between Hamlet and

The Culture of Edo   151

Macbeth and King Lear? Come to think of it, the quintessential art of the Edo era was the ukiyo-e woodblock print, right? Those too have no dimensionality. They're beautiful, of course. They have wonderful composition and splendid use of color. I think every print by Suzuki Harunobu (1725–1770) is just magnificent. But look at any ten pieces by him and try to tell me what kind of personality he had—if he was a troubled soul, that kind of thing. You can't do it. All you can do is thrill at the gracefulness of his curves and the colors he uses. In a similar way, Edo literature lacks universality.

Shiba   In the end, there's just social circumstances without many people. Duty is a social circumstance in which human emotions have no place. So when dire circumstances force human emotions to come out, they clash with duty, and that creates drama. But when human emotions erupt one sees the nitty-gritty of human beings, so it is only then when we get a sense of the person as a three-dimensional reality.

Keene   Another thing to keep in mind is that the pace of life during the Edo period was unimaginably slow. When something happened, people would talk about it for decades. Consider, for example, the odd Hungarian who styled himself Maurice, Count de Benyovszky (1746–1786). It's hard to say which of the stories about him are true, but supposedly he was captured by the Russian army during a war, traversed the wilds of Siberia in chains, started a riot while in exile in Kamchatka, stole a boat, and escaped to Japan. This guy sent a letter from Amami Oshima[11] to the head of the trade house at Dejima in Nagasaki, telling him to be careful because the Russians were planning to attack Japan. Looking back we now know that Russia was in no state to do such a thing, but the Japanese argued about this as a serious national defense issue for twenty years. If something like that

11. An island in Kagoshima prefecture between Kyushu and Okinawa.

152   Chapter 8

happened today, I imagine it would blow over in a few days. Or consider the incident of the forty-seven ronin we were discussing earlier. I understand wanting to dress that up and dramatize it right after the event, but it went on for fifty, sixty years. People kept finding new angles on the story, minor variations on the same theme. The version of the story that's most often read today was written forty-five years after the incident. It's hard to believe people could remain interested for so long.

Shiba   Interesting, isn't it? And the story was expressed in so many genres. There are the kabuki plays of course, but professional storytellers tell that tale too. They've even created spinoff stories about it. Like the one about Kanzaki Yogoro bowing and apologizing after being scolded by a stableman when crossing the mountains in Hakone. There's no way to know if those events took place, but people did get a lot of enjoyment out of them, over and over again.

Keene   One can only assume that there wasn't much happening during the Edo period.

Shiba   I think one year's worth of the society section from a modern newspaper would have provided enough material to last the whole 270 years of the Edo era. Too much, even. From movies and television shows you get the impression that people were killing and being killed in swordfights all over the place, but nothing like that really happened. The Edo era was remarkably murder-free.

Keene   I imagine that if Chikamatsu were alive today, he'd have so much to write about he wouldn't know where to start.

Shiba   I doubt he'd last as a novelist for more than a few years. [Laughs]

Two Eccentrics: Shiba Kokan and Hiraga Gennai

Keene I'm very interested in Shiba Kokan (1747–1818) and Hiraga Gennai (1728–1779). What I find most interesting about them is that they were born in this peculiar time that was the Edo period. I don't think I would find them so surprising if they had been born today, or in the Warring States period, mainly because during the Edo period, the Tokugawa shogunate emphasized conformity so heavily. The Tokugawa clan had a particular notion of how all Japanese should be, and they used Confucianism to preserve their own authority. Any Japanese who could accept that would advance smoothly, so even warriors could attain social prominence. But surely there were social outcasts who didn't fit in. Most people like that ran the risk of being noticed and labeled suspect by official censors. But there was one exception—the eccentrics. If you were an eccentric, you were okay. It's just like the way high school students were viewed in prewar Japan. I guess you could call them the eccentrics of their time, while junior high school and university students were considered "normal."

Shiba I'm stunned that you know that, that high school students under the old system were considered to be ostentatious oddballs.

Keene Hiraga Gennai in particular was a true eccentric. He was a samurai of the Takamatsu domain[12], and he retained connections with that region his entire life. He was unlike anyone else, though. If you read his biography you learn that this one person wrote plays, made pottery, wrote political essays, developed a non-flammable cloth using asbestos, discovered mines ... He just did everything. There are two portraits of him, each with a completely different expression. They don't look anything alike. In one he's very fat while in the other he's very thin, so it's hard to form a mental picture of him. And of all

---

12. Modern-day Kagawa prefecture.

the things he did, almost none of it amounted to anything. He wrote a puppet theater play called *Shinrei Yaguchi no Watashi* (Miracle at the Yaguchi Ferry) that's somewhat interesting, but the novel is just awful. He painted a *bijin-ga* portrait of a woman that's at the Kobe Namban Art Museum[13], and while I suppose it's of historical interest, it isn't particularly good. But the reason I find him so interesting is that he was such a complex person, so different from the image we have of someone living in the Edo period. He's like the antithesis of that time.

Shiba Kokan was also quite eccentric. For example, he once sent a notice of his own death to various people, long before he actually died, then complained when nobody came to pay their respects. When you read his writings, they have a strangely contemporary feel to them, because he's so filled with contradictions just like people today are.

I think that the more people contradict themselves, the more interesting they are. A person's contradictions reveal what they're thinking about. I mean, what's interesting about a follower of Zhu Xi just passing on the teachings of Zhu Xi? But with Shiba Kokan, we see him one day writing, "Buddhism is worthless, it's garbage," then on another day writing about what a wonderful religion it is. Sure, those statements contradict each other, but each is quite interesting. Kokan would change like the wind, adamantly opposing something one day, and wholeheartedly supporting it the next. And to think that such a person lived in the times he did, when consistency was so highly praised. His paintings wouldn't be considered to have much artistic merit today, but he had such an adventurous spirit, and he was so incredibly curious about new things. He considered himself connected to all things, and so blocked out nothing. He even accepted things that came from a very different world than his own, and that was rare in the Edo period. He's usually referred to as a Western studies scholar, but many people

---

13. Now called the Kobe City Museum.

knew far more about the West than he did. So I don't think that's what made him such a great man.

Shiba Kokan's greatest achievement was presenting the findings of others in clear, enjoyable language, which he disseminated in books with interesting illustrations. It's possible that he developed some of the techniques that are still used for illustrating books today. Of course, artistic illustrations existed long before he did, as far back as the *Tale of Genji Scroll*. But he was the first to produce illustrations aimed at giving readers a mental image of the text. He was clearly influenced by his Western studies. He read Dutch books, and they'd have these interesting characters in the illustrations, like the maps of the Netherlands that always used a woman to represent the wind ...

Shiba   And the swimming whales ...

Keene   And interesting houses. He learned about all these things, and decided Japan should have books with illustrations like that, too. So neither he nor Hiraga were first-rate academics, nor were they first-rate literary figures. But they were first-rate human beings. They were very interesting people of the best sort.

Shiba   I think the point you started out with—about how only eccentrics were allowed to deviate from the otherwise narrow-minded Edo systems—is very important. That is indeed how we should look at it. Back then, some people were considered to be outside the mainstream—people like doctors, Buddhist monks, and Shinto priests who were positioned outside the standard samurai–farmer–craftsman–merchant social hierarchy. But Gennai and Kokan were samurai, and they were supposed to fit within the hierarchy. So I wonder what it means that they were accepted as eccentrics. That seems to indicate some kind of social acknowledgement of "eccentric" status. I wonder if Japan had some sort of tradition that separated true eccentrics from

156   Chapter 8

those who were just playing the part.

Now that I think about it, we Japanese do seem to admire our eccentrics. But it still seems like in the Edo period such behavior would have landed you in jail. There must have been some kind of tacit reason for allowing the exceptions. So what allowed Hiraga Gennai to get away with things he could have been arrested for? Was there some kind of psychological habit that led people to position him outside the reach of law and normal customs?

Keene   Perhaps even rigid societies like Edo Japan need an outlet like that. In older times, both in Japan and medieval Europe, people like him became monks. That's probably all they could do. But in more recent eras exceptional people stopped cloistering themselves away. If they could adopt the title of "eccentric," if they could label themselves that way, then they could get away with things that otherwise would have been unacceptable. Shiba Kokan lived a very self-centered life, in many ways the opposite of what was expected in the Edo period, but he was never convicted of anything, or even reprimanded for his behavior. I guess people of the time figured, why bother?

Shiba   That's why to be an eccentric you had to have some kind of exceptional insight or knowledge that set you far beyond the average person. If you did, then in very rare cases you might be labeled as a vent for an otherwise closed society.

Keene   As a rare exception, yes.

Motoori Norinaga – Conclusion

Shiba   It's almost time to wrap up our conversation, which I think up to this point has pursued the general theme of "just what is Japanese culture?" Japan doesn't export its culture well, by which I mean, there's such a thing as geographical environment in world history, and

I think Japan is a place where things collect. Things that drained out of China accumulated here, for example. These things collect in our culture, and our language, and even in our architecture, in places like the Shoso-in treasure house. But it's hard to imagine things being pushed from Japan into China, ideas coming from here and affecting Chinese thought because they're needed there. If Japan had a bit more national territory I imagine it would try to accommodate all the cultures of the world, but we're a bit too small for that.

Keene The Japanese always seem to be preoccupied with the question of what is "Japanese." I think it's been that way since long ago. The scholars of *kokugaku* nativist studies were particularly concerned with this, I'd say. People like Motoori Norinaga, who went searching for a "pure" Japanese language and ended up writing in a language completely unlike the one he used in daily life—one that avoided all "impure" words that came from other countries, and so was very strange and unnatural. Even today the Japanese seem concerned with how "Japanese" things will remain in the future, and whether those characteristics might disappear entirely. But as long as there are Japanese people in the world, I'm quite convinced that the character of Japan will remain in all forms of its expression. It's when you become too concerned about this and go out of your way to bring out the "Japanese-ness" in things that you end up with something unnatural, like Motoori did.

Shiba I agree completely. And that's the perfect note to end this conversation on—that if you try too hard, you end up with a mess. Not that I'm going to call Motoori's works a mess, but they are indeed unnatural. Ever since I was a child, I've found—and I even told [literary critic] Kobayashi Hideo this—I've always found his writing unbearable. Reading him leaves me in a state of psychological discomfort. Do you not feel the same?

Keene   Exactly the same.

Shiba   Well that's a relief. Sometimes I worry that I'm the only one.

Keene   I'm sure he was a wonderful scholar, but his writings are just... well, strange.

Shiba   His *Tamakatsuma*, for example, is like a piece of fine handiwork, something to be viewed but not really enjoyed. Writing is supposed to be at least somewhat engaging, no matter who wrote it, right? But I get zero enjoyment out of *Tamakatsuma*.

Keene   When considering the future of Japanese culture too, remember that while today we consider all these new expressways and highrise apartment buildings to be unsightly, one hundred years from now people will look back on them with fond nostalgia. Just recently, I was with someone who looked at an ordinary light bulb and mentioned how it reminded him of the past. When I asked him why, he said the home he lives in now is completely lit with fluorescent bulbs, so incandescent bulbs had become nostalgic for him. I suppose that isn't at all related to ancient Japanese culture, but it shows that, given enough time, pretty much anything can inspire nostalgia. From our perspective, it seems like automobiles will always be with us. But if some new invention completely replaces them, where does that leave our expressways? Maybe they'll become something unimaginably beautiful. We could plant them over with flowers. [Laughs]

Shiba   Well now there's a grand scheme. But I suppose the point is, there's no use in worrying.

Afterword

When I was first approached with the suggestion for these conversations with Mr. Shiba, I was of course quite honored. Yet at the same time I felt a bit apprehensive, because I had spent years immersed in the world of ancient Japanese literature, and had never read any of Shiba's novels. Not that I feared I would be tested on the Shiba corpus, but I was sure that my lack of knowledge would somehow be exposed. Should the organizer suddenly ask which of his books I enjoyed the most, for example, I wasn't sure how I could answer that.

Shiba agreed to our meeting while I was still wavering over how to respond. Not only that, but I was told that as a condition, he had requested that I not read any of his books beforehand. This resolved my only concern, so I replied that I would gladly participate.

When I was informed of the plans for three separate meetings—one each in Nara, Kyoto, and Osaka—I was afraid we would run out of things to discuss, because I had never engaged in such a long dialogue. To be honest, I was also slightly wary of Shiba, afraid that he would ask things like, "In the period of Japan's history we call 'Meiji,' there was a Japanese author named Natsume Soseki. Have you heard of him?" But all such fears were alleviated after less than five minutes of conversation, and we ended up talking like old friends. It was a delightful opportunity to discuss interesting "discoveries" I had recently made, and to have a sounding board for new theories. Far from running out of things to talk about, new topics arose naturally one after the next.

Clearly both of us like to talk, and our discussions may come across as a long conversation between two people who happened to be sitting next to each other on a seven- or eight-hour train ride. This places the reader as a fellow passenger sitting nearby and listening in, and if that describes the feeling you had while reading this dialogue, I sincerely hope that you enjoyed the ride as much as we did.

Donald Keene

Photo taken in 1971 at the Ginkakuji temple, courtesy of CHUOKORON-SHINSHA, L

About the Authors

Donald Keene

Donald Keene was born in New York in 1922. He graduated from Columbia University in 1942 and immediately entered the Navy Japanese Language School. He served as a translator and interpreter during World War II. Afterwards, he obtained a doctoral degree from Columbia. He first taught at Cambridge University in 1948–53. He spent 1953–55 at Kyoto University, then became a professor at Columbia in 1955. Since then, he has published over 50 books related to Japan's literature and culture in Japanese and English. He received Japan's Medal of Culture in 2008.

Shiba Ryotaro

Shiba Ryotaro was born in Osaka in 1923, and graduated from the Mongolian department at the Osaka Foreign Language School. In 1960, while working as a newspaper reporter, he received the Naoki Prize for his first novel *Fukuro no Shiro* (Castle of Owls), after which he became a full-time novelist. He has received many other awards, including the Japan Art Academy's Imperial Award, for his many historical works such as *Kukai no Fukei* (Kukai the Universal: Scenes from his Life). He received the Order of Culture in 1993. Other main works include *Ryoma ga Yuku* (Ryoma Goes his Way), *Kaido o Yuku* (On the Highway), *Kono Kuni no Katachi* (The Form of Our Country), and *Saka no Ue no Kumo* (Clouds above the Hill: A historical novel of the Russo-Japanese War). He died in February 1996.

Index

A

Akechi Mitsuhide, 43–44
Akiyama Saneyuki, 28, 69
Akiyama Yoshifuru, 69
Alcock, Rutherford, 123
Amakusa Shiro, 133
Amaro, 21
Amaterasu, 141
Amitabha Buddha, 51, 89, 90
An Lushan, 130
Ando Shoeki, 91
Aoto Zoshi Hana no Nishikie. see
    Shiranami Gonin Otoko
Arase Susumu, 115
Asano Takumi no Kami, 146–148
Ashikaga Yoshimasa, 47–48, 56, 58,
    125–128, 131
Ashikaga Yoshimitsu, 49, 52, 56–58,
    126-127

B

Bai Juyi, 24
Baishi Wenji, 24

Basho, 6, 11, 23–25, 141, 145, 148
Bellecourt. *see* Duchesne
Blind Emperor, The, 111
Bukegiri Monogatari, 146

C

Chamberlain, Basil Hall, 120–123
Chikamatsu Monzaemon, 11, 85, 134,
    139, 145, 149–150, 152
Chunhyangjeon, 19
Clark, William S., 115
Claudel, Paul, 12
Confucius, 79, 85
Count de Benyovszky, Maurice, 151

D

Daudet, Alphonse, 111
Dengyo Daishi. *see* Saicho
Doeff, Hendrik, 106–107, 109
Dogen, 38
Du Fu, 24–25, 128–129
Duchesne, 117

E

Eikoku Sakuron, 119

*Epochs of Chinese and Japanese
Art*, 130

F

Fenollosa, Ernest, 120–123, 130

Five Years in Japan, 114

Forty-Seven Ronin, The, 144,
146-148, 152

Franklin, Benjamin, 27

Fuchida Mitsuo, 73–74

Fujino Tsunesaburo, 104

Fujiwara no Teika, 128, 130

Fujiwara Seika, 87–88

Fukuba Bisei, 97

Fukuchi Gen'ichiro, 92

Fukuzawa Yukichi, 100, 102–103

Funa Benkei, 124

Furuta Oribe, 60

G

Gido Shushin, 39

H

Hachijo Toshihito, Prince, 62

Hachinoki, 125

Hagihara Nobutoshi, 117, 120

Hamamatsu Chunagon Monogatari, 18

Harris, Townsend, 123

Harunobu, 151

Hayashi Razan, 141

Hearn, Lafcadio, 115, 122

Hegel, 123

Hepburn, James Curtis, 101

Hino Tomiko, 51

Hiraga Gennai, 153, 155–156

Hirata Atsutane, 97, 138

*Historical Grammar of Japanese,
An,* 124

History of Japanese Literature, A, 44

Hojoki, 137

Honcho Niju Fuko, 136

Honda Toshiaki, 90–91, 93

Hong Xiuquan, 133

Hosokawa Gracia, 43

Hosokawa Tadaoki, 43–44

Huiguo, 34, 37

I

Ichihara Toyota, 12

Ichijo Kaneyoshi, 55

Ihara Saikaku. *see* Saikaku

Ikkyu Sojun, 38–39

Imoseyama Onna Teikin (The Teaching for Women), 111–112

Ine, 110

Ippin Issho Shinso no Kajin, 29

Ito Genboku, 104

Ito Hirobumi, 29

Izumi Kyoka, 71

J

Japan: A Short Cultural History, 124

Japanese Discovery of Europe, The, 90

K

Kada no Azumamaro, 18

Kagero Nikki (The Gossamer Years), 149–150

Kaifuso, 14, 16

Kaijo Hatsuden, 71

Kaizuka Shigeki, 129

Kajin no Kigu, 29–30

Kakiemon, 59

Kamo no Chomei, 137

Kano Eitoku, 57

Kanzaki Yogoro, 152

Karaki Junzo, 49

Kato Kiyomasa, 88

Katsu Kaishu, 91–92, 126

Katsura Kogoro, 146

Kawakami Tetsutaro, 104

Kawatake Mokuami, 144

Keika. *see* Huiguo

Kenko, 53–54, 56

Ki no Tsurayuki, 21, 23

Kido Takayoshi, 92

Kira Yoshinaka, 147–148

Kobayakawa Hideaki, 65

Kobayashi Hideo, 157

Kobo Daishi. *see* Kukai

Koizumi Yakumo. *see* Hearn, Lafcadio

Kojiki, 139

Kokin Wakashu, 20, 23–24

Kokinshu. see Kokin Wakashu

Kuga Katsunan, 27

Kukai, 31-37

Kukai Zenshu, 31

Kumagai Naozane, 67

Kurimoto Joun, 118

Kyo'unshu, 38

Kyui, 52

L

Laozi, 127, 129

Les Contes du lundi, 111

Li He, 129

Lin Biao, 22

M

Maeda Toshiie, 87

Makura no Soshi, 18

Mamiya Rinzo, 110

Man'yoshu, 14, 18, 20, 23

Mao Zedong, 81

Masaoka Shiki, 26–28, 69

Matsumoto Jun. *see* Matsumoto Ryojun

Matsumoto Ryojun, 112–114

Matsunaga Teitoku, 44, 145

Matsuo Basho. *see* Basho

Meckel, 65

Meigetsuki, 128

Mencius, 79, 85, 134

Meyerbeer, Giacomo, 111

Minamoto no Yoritomo, 67, 131

Minamoto no Yoshitsune, 131

Moltke, 65

Monday Tales. *see* Les Contes du lundi

Moraes, Wenceslau-de, 115–116

Mori, 39

Mori Ogai, 97, 100, 116

Motoori Norinaga, 30, 78, 157

Muqi Fachang, 130

Murasaki Shikibu, 20, 23, 149

Murata Zoroku. *see* Omura Masujiro

N

Nagai Kafu, 144

Nagumo Chuichi, 73

Nakamura Naokatsu, 49

Napoleon, 23, 64, 117–118

Napoleon III, 117–118

Natsume Soseki, 26, 161

Nebiki no Kadomatsu, 134

Nero, 48

Nichiren, 35

Nihon Shoki, 13, 139

Nishi Amane, 97, 98, 100–101, 103

Nogi Maresuke, 69

O

O Bon-odori em Tokushima, 116

Oda Nobunaga, 43, 55, 57–58, 80, 131

Ogata Koan, 101–102, 104, 107

Ogata Tomio, 104

Oguri Kozukenosuke, 118

Ogyu Sorai, 78

Oishi Kuranosuke, 146

Okakura Tenshin, 121

Oku no Hosomichi (The Narrow Road to Oku), 24–25, 149

Okubo Toshimichi, 131–132

Omura Masujiro, 101–103

Otomo no Yakamochi, 23

Otori Keisuke, 104

Otori Ranzaburo, 104–105

Ozaki Koyo, 28

P

Park Chung-hee, 19

Pompe, 112-116

R

Rai San'yo, 83

Rakuchu Rakugai screen paintings, 57–58

Rembrandt, 60

Rhee, Syngman, 19

Rinzai, 38

Robespierre, 66

Roches, Leon, 117

S

Saemon. *see* Sayaka

Saicho, 37

Saigo Takamori, 119–120, 131–132, 146

Saigyo, 23

Saikaku, 11, 136, 145–146

Sakamoto Ryoma, 91, 126

Sakuma Shozan, 94

Sansom, George, 123–124

Sato Norikiyo, 23

Satow, Ernest, 117–120, 122

Sayaka, 68

Sei Shonagon, 18, 23

Self-Help, 27

Sen no Rikyu, 59–60

Sesshu, 54

Shakespeare, 150

Shiba Kokan, 153–156

Shiba Ryokai, 113–114

Shijing, 18

Shimanaka Hoji, 10

Shinju Ten no Amijima, 149

Shinran, 35, 88–90

Shinrei Yaguchi no Watashi, 154

Shiranami Gonin Otoko, 144

Shodo Geijutsu, 31

Shotoku, Prince, 13, 17

Siddhartha Gautama, 32

Siebold, Philipp Franz von, 108-113

Smiles, Samuel, 27

Sogi, 53–54, 56

Sudo Nansui, 29, 30

Sugawara no Michizane, 16, 21

Sun Tzu, 63

Suzuki Harunobu. *see* Harunobu

T

Taira no Kiyomori, 131

Taira no Shigemori, 131

Tajo-Takon, 28, 30

Takahashi Kageyasu, 110

Taketori Monogatari, 20

Tale of Genji, The, 17–20, 53, 122

Tale of Genji Scroll, The, 53, 155

Tamakatsuma, 158

Tanizaki Junichiro, 144

Theory of *akunin shoki*, 88–89

Toba, Retired Emperor, 23

Togo Heihachiro, 28

Tokai Sanshi, 29

Tokugawa Ieyasu, 44, 55, 62–63, 65, 132

Tokugawa Tsunayoshi, 132–133

Tokugawa Yoshimune, 132

Tosa Nikki, 21

Toyotomi Hideyoshi, 42, 57–58, 65, 131, 132

Tsuji Zennosuke, 49

Tsurezuregusa, 54, 123

U

Uesugi Kenshin, 57

Uso Manpitsu Ryokusadan, 29

V

Vairocana Buddha, 32, 41

Valéry, Paul, 12

W

Waley, Arthur, 122

Wang Zhi, 72

Wellesly, Arthur. *see* Wellington

Wellington, 23, 64

Wright, Frank-Lloyd, 116

X

Xavier, Francis, 41, 42, 85–86

Xuanzong, Emperor, 130

Y

Yamawaki Toyo, 77–78

Yamazaki Ansai, 94

Yang, Emperor, 16–17

Yang Guifei, 130

Yokoi Shonan, 91–92

Yoshida Kenko. *see* Kenko

Yoshida Shoin, 134

Yukawa Hideki, 21

Z

Zeami, 52, 126

Zhang Liang, 22

Zhuang Zhou, 127, 129

Zoshi, 78

（英文版）日本人と日本文化（『ドナルド・キーン著作集 第九巻 世界のなかの日本文化』所収）
The People and Culture of Japan: Conversations Between Donald Keene and Shiba Ryotaro

2018年7月27日　第1刷発行
2019年5月27日　第2刷発行

著　者　ドナルド・キーン
　　　　司馬遼太郎
訳　者　トニー・ゴンザレス
発行所　一般財団法人 出版文化産業振興財団
　　　　〒101-0051 東京都千代田区神田神保町3-12-3
　　　　電話　03-5211-7282（代）
　　　　ホームページ　http://www.jpic.or.jp/

印刷・製本所　株式会社ウイル・コーポレーション

定価はカバーに表示してあります。
本書の無断複写（コピー）、転載は著作権法の例外を除き、禁じられています。

Printed in Japan

© 1972, 2013 by Donald Keene, Uemura Yoko and Shiba Ryotaro Memorial Foundation
ISBN 978-4-916055-57-6<HBK>
ISBN 978-4-86658-048-7<PBK>